seek the face of god

THE IGNATIAN IMPULSE SERIES ✠ IHS

seek the face of god

discovering the power of your images of god

Karl Frielingsdorf

ave maria press AmP Notre Dame, IN

Scripture quotations are from the *New Revised Standard Version Bible,* copyright © 1993 and 1989 by the Division of Christian Education of the National Council of Churches of Christ in the U.S.A. Used by permission. All rights reserved.

First published as *Gottesbilder Wie sie krank machen, wie sie heilen* in Germany in ©2004 by Echter Verlag.

Translated by Albert Wimmer

© 2006 Ave Maria Press, Inc.

www.avemariapress.com

ISBN–10: 1-59471-037-6
ISBN–13: 978-1-59471-037-7

Cover and text design by Brian C. Conley

Printed and bound in the United States of America.

Library of Congress Cataloging-in-Publication Data
Frielingsdorf, Karl.
  [Gottesbilder Wie sie krank machen, wie sie heilen English]
  Seek the face of God : discovering the power of your images of God / Karl Frielingsdorf.
    p. cm. — (The Ignatian impulse)
  Includes bibliographical references.
  ISBN-13: 978-1-59471-037-7 (pbk.)
  ISBN-10: 1-59471-037-6 (pbk.)
  1. God. 2. God—Face. 3. Spiritual life—Catholic Church. I. Title. II. Series.

BT103.F7513 2006
231—dc22
                    2005027097

C ONTENTS

INTRODUCTION

The purpose of this book is to stimulate and encourage us to reflect on our many and varied images of God. For the most part, these images originated in our childhood. If we are willing to consider them anew we will be able not only to unmask those images of God that are unhealthy, but also to know and love Jesus better, and through him, to know and love the one true God whom he has revealed to us.

Time and again we come to the realization that our words about God as loving or merciful do not match the image of God that we may carry with us, images of God as a tormentor, a petty bean-counter, an arbitrary tyrant, or a merciless judge. In most cases, the sources of these images are deep-seated, negative experiences from the relationships of childhood. As children we may have subconsciously transferred to God the negative personality traits of our parents. In the worst instances, the good news can be transformed into a threatening message that conveys a demonic image of God. Christianity is thus perverted into a magical superstition.

The revival of demonic images of God in our contemporary world is striking. We see it in the rituals of occult movements, in Satanic cults, or in astrological consultations to predict the future. But sadly, we also see it in religious congregations and sects leaning toward fundamentalism. In this kind of environment, the repressed, negative images of

God that lie dormant can be activated even in people with a sound religious formation. Such images can lead to many forms of unhealthy behavior. Although groups like these talk expressly about God, they do not provide a way to encounter the true God who is revealed in the Bible. Instead, they worship evil spirits that ultimately lead to superstition.

In my discussion and in the stories of life and faith that follow in this book, four negative images of God will surface most frequently: God as a judge who punishes, God in the guise of death, God as an accountant, and God as a demanding taskmaster. In most cases, negative, unhealthy images of God develop from focusing on one aspect or one image of God and making it the dominant, absolute image. No one aspect of God can be an absolute. Rather, only a multitude of symbols and designations can begin to provide a somewhat adequate description of God. God is not uniform but multiform; there are more dimensions of God than human beings are capable of fathoming. For instance, the images of God both as Mother and as Father are capable of conveying the reality of God expressed in the Bible. *Both are representations* that, despite their respective completeness, do not preclude the other image. When we consider all the possible ways of experiencing and describing God, we must come to recognize the fact that we will never be able to fully comprehend God. In the end, all of our language about God cannot change the fact that God is ultimately beyond our capacity to comprehend. Thus we are always in search of the true God.

The purpose of this book is to help readers discover ways to unmask any subconscious, demonic images of God and to replace them with positive and healing images of God. Throughout our endeavors, Ignatius of Loyola's "Rules for the Discernment of Spirits" from *The Spiritual Exercises* will prove to be an excellent tool for discovering images of God that either obstruct or promote life. As we will see from the process of the discernment of spirits, in the end, demonic or evil spirits create despair and internal unrest, while healthy and positive images ultimately provide internal peace and comfort.

We encounter the true God in our ardent longing and deepest desire for life and love. These primordial desires are affirmed and complemented by all the sources of God's revelation, most of all through Jesus Christ. Jesus reveals a God who is a benevolent and merciful Father, who takes care of his children like a loving Mother.

Through the discernment of spirits we are invited to trust the promises of the one true God who has unmistakably offered us the fullness of life from the moment when we were called by our Christian names for the first time in baptism. And we are invited again, as we were in our baptismal promises, to renounce evil, that is to renounce demonic images of God and to counter their life-denying and life-impeding messages with life-giving and life-promoting testimony. The resurrection to genuine life begins the very moment we let God touch and love us. In the following story, entitled "God's Lessons," God himself takes care of "discerning the spirits."

A little boy was eating some candy that he had taken without his mother's permission, but she caught him in the act. Being a pious woman intent on raising her children in the faith, she said to him:

"Listen, my dear son, don't you know that God is watching you all the time and notices everything you do?"

"Oh, Mom, of course I know that."

"Well then, didn't you realize that God was watching you when you were in the kitchen?"

"Of course he was watching me."

"And what do you think he was saying when he saw you sneaking into the candy jar?"

"Well, you know what he said? He said, 'My dear child, you and I are all alone in the kitchen, so go ahead and take two pieces of candy!'"

CHAPTER ONE

IS IT POSSIBLE TO PICTURE GOD?

Whenever we talk about God and the various images of God, we must begin with the awareness that so-called God language will never be able to produce the clarity we would like. God can be neither described nor defined. And yet, we speak of God as our opposite, as the one who is our source and the one toward whom we direct our lives and our faith. A picture painted by a ten-year-old girl expresses well the possibilities and limits of our human knowledge and language about God. The painting portrays a colorful landscape, depicting creation with its many fruits, flowers, and plants stretching toward the heavens. At the center of the picture there is a big empty chair. Three crosses are etched into its seat. Underneath the painting, the little girl wrote, with uncanny certainty: "Here is God sitting on his throne."

Even with the certainty of faith, we recognize our simultaneous inability to draw a specific picture of God. The three crosses confirm the fact that there is no language that we can learn that will adequately describe God. Like people who cannot read or write, the best we can do is merely confirm, with the help of some sign like the crosses, our belief that God constitutes a reality in our lives and that he sustains our lives.

Frequently, when we speak of and about God we rely on experiences that are not immediately recognizable as religious experiences. God, of course, is not limited to these religious contexts, nor to any reality that our senses and our minds are capable of comprehending. That is why we are unable to form a concept of God that corresponds to the reality of God. God is not like all the other objects of our experience that we are able to define.

We are unable to comprehend God or speak of him directly; we can only speak of him indirectly. We can see our existence as a metaphor: it is filled with and reflective of his works, it points to God. Just as Jesus spoke in parables, we are ultimately able to speak of God by viewing the things and events occurring in our lives as signs and symbols pointing beyond themselves toward an entirely different, infinitely transcendent, and yet truly present reality. It is a reality at the root of our existence. Those things that we recognize as signs and symbols are directed toward it and partake in it, but in finite form.

These experiences of and with God are as varied as our lives. Any time we speak of what God is like, we also express at the same time that God is not like anything else. God is incomparable. That is why descriptions of God as infinite, unconditional, unchangeable, immortal, ineffable, and so forth, must always be accompanied by "not this way," i.e., the realization of how inadequate these descriptive adjectives really are in spite of their positive meaning. The God of the gospels is not a God who can be conceptualized logically based on an ideal reality, but is a God who reveals himself and who is experienced through the kinds of personal encounters attested to in the scriptures. Throughout these historical self-revelations, God reveals himself in human experiences as Yahweh: the God who is one, who is forever present, faithful, and loving. Yahweh is the one who created the world, and from whose love all reality originates, forever new like a spring that never stops flowing. In him the world will reach its fulfillment at the end of times. And yet, in spite of this revelation, God remains an unfathomable mystery.

In the New Testament, God uniquely reveals himself by assuming human form in the person of Jesus Christ. Through Jesus, we can talk to and experience God who is part of our reality. But despite becoming this incarnated Jesus, God is not an object of our knowledge. Even here, the mystery remains. To us, the human Jesus becomes a sacrament of God. In him the capacity of our world to be a metaphor reaches its culmination. In everything he is and everything he does he points to God whom he calls his Father; through him we are able to experience God (Jn 14:9).

It is against this background of the limited ways in which we are able to recognize and speak about God that we can begin to speak about images of God. Josef Auer described an image as the "spiritual medium in which and through which the vital encounter between a religious human being and his or her God takes place." A personal image of God represents and expresses the power within us that is capable of sustaining and inspiring our lives most deeply. Yet at the same time it is also capable of obstructing and burdening us.

To those who have been raised with some degree of religious education, the varied images of God that were learned in early childhood are fundamentally important. They form the basic patterns of our feelings, our thoughts, and our conduct, whether they are close to reality or far removed from it, whether they function as obstacles to growth or as forces enhancing it. The images of God that shape us are frequently difficult to identify because they influence and steer our lives largely on a subconscious level. Subconscious images of God never correspond completely with conscious images. In fact, they are frequently at odds with one another. For instance, some people speak of God as a benevolent and merciful Father, yet, deep inside themselves, they are dominated by a merciless, demanding God who requires achievement. Thus, the image of God we consciously proclaim is not always the one operative in our lives. Instead, it is the subconscious image of God that ultimately determines and forms us.

Imagine for a moment an image of God that is complete. This *primordial image* of God would contain all the beauty of creation and the grace of salvation. It would express God as the beginning and the end of all things. It might be likened to a gigantic mosaic composed of an uncountable numbers of tiles—i.e., all those different and unique images of God that defy an internal unity. Although we might be able to imagine such an image, this primordial image of God will always be incomplete. Although it may contain an unfathomable dimension of depth, it will remain only an image in need of constant augmentation.

God is sometimes described as a coincidence of contradictions. This perspective is manifested in many ways. We experience God as both near and distant. We refer to God as the one who is both farthest removed from us and as our neighbor. We experience God as the silent one who nevertheless speaks to us through all things. We experience God as merciful and benevolent, but also as the one who seeks justice relentlessly. We encounter God as the nameless one with a thousand names, or as the holy one who nevertheless permits atrocities and crimes.

Artistic portrayals of the incarnate Son of God, Jesus Christ, also illustrate the many different views of God. Compare, for instance, the various portrayals of Jesus. He is the Good Shepherd in the paintings in the early Christian catacombs, the ruler of the world in Romanesque art, the tortured and disfigured one in the magnificent altar tryptic by Matthias Grünewald at Saint Anthony's Monastery in Alsace, and the victim of the Holocaust portrayed by twentieth–century artists. From both a theological and psychological perspective we must always remember this principle: human beings are incapable of fully recognizing and comprehending the fullness of God. All we can do is recognize and comprehend the individual aspects that form the great mosaic. The depth of God's totality, however, is and will forever remain a mystery. The writings of both the Old and the New Testament reveal a variety of images of God. Especially in the New Testament, the dynamic nature of God is revealed in the relationship between Father, Son, and Holy Spirit.

Unhealthy idols or demonic images of God originate when an image of God is one-sided, when a partial aspect of God is rendered absolute and viewed as if it were complete. Drawing from the description in the Book of Revelation, Karl Rahner described demons as "spirits that damage both body and life," as "harmful and corrupting," and as "spirits who lead us into sin." Originally, God created them as good spirits but, after deciding to turn against their creator, they became evil. Even though Christian faith proclaims that salvation through Jesus Christ ultimately overcomes evil, the demons nevertheless keep on corrupting humanity and causing it harm. They try to alienate human beings from God; they act as negative spirits who lead us to practice superstition. They pretend to be the true God.

Proceeding from humanity's affliction with original sin, the concept of demonic images of God recognizes that evil affects human beings from the moment they are born. Based on positive and negative childhood experiences, demonic images of God take shape alongside positive images during early childhood, images that are frequently considered to be reflective of the true God. As demonic images of God, they are capable of clandestinely exercising their power all the way to adulthood.

In contrast to these demonic images, the primordial Christian image of God has three key dimensions:

1. God is a *personal* God in whose image human beings are created. We encounter this God in others, especially in Jesus, the incarnate Son of God. Because we are created in the image of God, every human being possesses an indelible, inner core of goodness, a divine fountain of life that exists in the depths of the human self from which the human dynamic of continual creation unfolds. In this existential depth of our personhood, we touch not only the core of our being, but God as well, who

dwells in us in a special way (1 Cor 3:16; Jn 7: 37 ff.; 14:20; 15:1-8). This fountain of life originates from God and exists as a positive disposition toward a life of fullness. Even if we should turn away from God through sin, wishing to be "creators" in our own right, there is always the possibility to turn back to the true source of creation.

2. God is *universal*, transcending the world and existing independently of it. He is subject neither to the laws of nature nor to ordinary causality.

3. God is the *entirely different one*, the truly other, an unattainable mystery that no human being will ever be able either to fathom or to penetrate.

These three components complement one another and contribute significantly to the development of a personal relationship with the God of the Christian faith.

C H A P T E R   T W O

CHILDREN'S IMAGES OF GOD

Researchers in the psychology of religion point out that our image of God is formed during the first couple of years of life, and that it is influenced by the socio-cultural environment.

Until a child is three or four years old, he or she "thinks" in terms of pictures and symbols; a child's logic is dictated by the *logic of these images*. Even during subsequent developmental stages, up to his or her sixth or seventh year, a child's thought processes are still determined by concrete imagery: *thoughts* about God are preceded by *pictures* of God. The image of God is a creative achievement by the child, even if the elements of religious imagery and imagination are imparted to the child by his or her social and cultural environment. The potential for active participation in the formation of these images is found in the child's power of imagination, that is to say, in his or her ability to create internal pictures.

If stereotypical images of God are imparted to the child at too early an age, there is a risk of overly determining and narrowing the child's imagination. Thus, it will be advisable to allow children to picture in their minds how they imagine God might look. Telling them, "you must not picture God in this way," fails to show the child the way to God. Instead, it is more helpful to encourage a child's ideas, to discuss them with the child, and to expand on them by asking probing questions. What matters throughout this process is that the child comes to the realization that his or her image of God will always need to be expanded, ultimately remaining open-ended because the true God will always be greater than any image representing him.

As they attempt to form an image of God, children are bound to connect their idea of God with the concrete experiences garnered from their environment, particularly those connected to the principal persons in their lives. Therefore, their early childhood experiences with their mothers and fathers are essential components in the formation of their perceptions of God. In particular, the experience of a mother who is all-encompassing, attentive, and dependable is important. A child's earliest experiences are of being embraced and encompassed by an omnipotent entity. This sense of total dependence is experienced first while still in the mother's womb. The mother has the power to give life to the child or not. She accepts the child or she rejects it, she embraces it lovingly or she neglects it. Thus, a mother can be perceived as a child's first god, or at least as a child's first symbol of God. As soon as the father becomes a more tangible presence in the interactive relationship between mother and child, the mother, as the child's initially absolute image of God, is rendered somewhat relative. From then on, she no longer functions as an all-encompassing image. Instead, the mother now becomes a symbol of something even greater that the child is looking for, something hidden behind its mother.

This perception of the mother as the ultimate authority can be strengthened if parents and child are praying together. It is here that the child learns for the first time that his or her mother, too, has concerns and needs that cause her to turn to somebody higher, namely God. Conversely, the child may also learn that his or her mother expresses prayers of thanksgiving to a greater, more encompassing and embracing entity, namely God. God holds her life in his hands throughout all her activities.

It is interesting to note in this context that, at first, the mother embodies the child's entire world. Everything the child encounters occurs through the mother's intimate and personal involvement. A newborn child experiences the world exclusively through the medium of individual attention—the primordial experience of every human being— with the result that the primordially other is personalized. What this means is that the primordial encounter with the first other preconditions the *personal* nature of religious imagery. The mother as the first person with whom the child has developed a relationship is subsequently complemented and replaced by different persons, preserving at the same time, however, the fundamental nature of the structure of the original relationship with the mother.

Thus, the mother and the father together play a decisive but not exclusive role in the creation of a child's image of God. In today's world, grandparents play an increasingly important role in this respect, particularly if they take on childcare responsibilities for working parents, or if parents no longer practice their faith. To these are added caregivers in daycare facilities and pre-schools, relatives, clergy, catechists or Sunday school teachers, etc. Religious values are particularly effective if they are practiced by people that children both love and respect.

What we know about childhood from the study of psychology and sociology also applies to the religious development of a child, particularly to the formation of images of God. Learning how to imitate others in their religious practice and to identify with them is especially important for the child. The continual development of the image of God during early childhood represents a dynamic, holistic learning process.

The way in which primary caregivers deal with life, the way in which they conduct themselves throughout their daily lives, their ideas of what is meaningful and valuable are all formative for the child. The degree to which trust, love, hope, forgiveness, and confidence can be concretely experienced and felt in a child's life plays an integral role in religious formation. Prayer and other religious experiences, such as worship services, the way religious holidays like Christmas or Easter are observed, the place of feast days of patron saints, birthdays, or the celebration of the sacraments at different junctures of life, all play an important part in forming the child's image of God.

In the age of media saturation, even television programs are important in the religious formation of children, particularly with regard to the development of images of God. A typical illustration of this process is the genie a ten-year-old boy painted in order to express his image of God after watching a television program featuring a genie. The words the boy used as a comment on his picture drive home the impact television had on his idea of God: "One must fear God, because God is a spirit. I couldn't think of any other spirit to portray God."

The degree to which the social atmosphere, the environment, and the overall ambience to which a child is exposed when growing up are able to affect his or her images of God is illustrated by two pictures made by two German children: one painted by a little girl from the foothills of the Alps and the other by a little boy from Munich. The little girl had been painting familiar Alpine scenes with mountains, lakes, animals, trees, and meadows. She included the Trinity, the Blessed Mother, the angels, the saints, and people, incorporating them all into this environment without any hesitation whatsoever. The little boy from the big city painted his picture of God against a background of highrises, helicopters, and stickmen, an image that was strikingly cold and colorless in its reflection of the modern world and its technology.

The central problem encountered on the journey to discovering the true God arises from the fundamental fact that God's existence and essence cannot be comprehended or expressed through words. It is frequently difficult to accept this contradiction; the tension of living with it leads some to avoid the whole idea of interaction with God. Conversely, some fall into the trap of grasping only one aspect of God, portraying it as if it were a complete picture and creating a one-sided view of God.

A further complication arises from the fact that the conscious and subconscious images of God are at odds with one another in the imagination of everyone, even if this tension remains on the subconscious level. For instance, in his sermons, a priest may talk about a benevolent and merciful God who loves each person specifically and tenderly. However, subconsciously he may exclude himself from God's goodness and love. His fears and nightmares testify to a different, negative image of God, a miserly God who tortures him and rules his subconscious.

Children, too, may experience God as a contradiction if their parents raise them by invoking God's authority while at the same time failing to orient their own lives toward him and refraining from keeping his ways. Similar contradictions regarding the development of images of God may arise whenever parents have two contrasting images of God. These early images of God can be complemented or modified later on in their lives, not only by God's grace, but by new religious experiences and spiritual growth as well. Thus new images and new experiences of God can render old ones relative.

CHAPTER THREE

TRADITIONAL IMAGES
OF GOD

Whenever we consciously deal with our past, something new and creative is bound to happen. If we neglect the past, even unintentionally, we run the risk of allowing the past to shape the present, either directly or indirectly. The result is the repetition of old patterns. To be sure, a constructive scrutiny and examination must not be confused with destructive digging into one's past. This approach can lead to brooding, dreaming, self-pity, or perhaps even to a kind of scapegoating. All of these patterns obstruct rather than promote one's ability to live fully in the present. The reason for examining the past is to come to an acceptance of the positive as well as the negative aspects of what we have inherited from childhood and to employ those elements as building blocks in the formation of our future lives. The same goes for reflecting on the images of God developed during childhood, images that, rising from the subconscious, are capable of guiding and steering our religious life. Any time we fail to engage these images consciously, there is the danger that our Christian faith may develop into magical superstition accompanied by corresponding negative spirits.

The first step in discovering our individual subconscious views of God is to examine consciously the faith that our parents impressed upon us, along with its accompanying images of God. Although these images began with the emotional relationship we enjoyed with our primary caregivers, they are not easy to comprehend. Frequently, we adopt them without reflecting on them, and prevent ourselves from developing an individual and personal relationship with God. Our goal instead should be the kind of personal relationship with God that includes making decisions about and assuming responsibility for our own life.

Many Christians today have abandoned the faith impressed upon them by their family without ever personally engaging it. For many, when they left their families and went their separate ways, the faith of their childhood became merely a habit, something that ran parallel to their real lives. Once it became mere mimicry it was increasingly more and more irrelevant. In many cases, this process has led to a complete alienation from religion and to a form of spiritual isolation. Cutting one's parental ties has been paralleled by a separation from faith, the church, and even God.

Oftentimes it is not easy for other people involved in the decisions that affect our lives today to understand that seemingly adult decisions (such as marriage, divorce, changing jobs or professions, or laicization) can deal with old patterns established by or learned from one's parents. In such instances, it is possible that the consequences of these patterns can be feelings of guilt or disappointment. Unless they are

SEEK THE FACE OF GOD

confronted, the present decision and the subsequent new direction can end in failure. An additional reason for taking a conscious and close look at the history of one's personal faith is the fact that many people fail to notice that they transfer their basically negative attitude toward life, their fear, distrust, feeling of inferiority, etc., onto God and their relationship with him. They unconsciously blame God for causing their misery. Others who were subjected to humiliation and abuse during childhood may intuitively seek refuge in God, wishing that he would turn out to be the kind of "sweet Lord" who would make up for the absence of maternal or paternal tenderness and love. When we reach adulthood, such a childlike, one-sided faith, together with its corresponding images of God, needs to be tested and augmented in the face of the realities of life and the reality of God. Only then can we reach the goal of a personal relationship with the living God who is different from the God that was able to inspire and sustain us throughout childhood.

It will be useful, too, to become aware of the history of one's personal faith. Many priests and religious have found this helpful when trying to determine the many conscious and unconscious motives of their vocations. In the past, for example, it was not uncommon to dedicate children to God while they were still in their mothers' wombs, during a difficult delivery, or in the course of a severe illness. A variety of motives, external as well as hidden, can lead one to become a priest or enter a religious community. There may be a fear of closeness to other people and of relationships or a fear of sexuality; a fear of being abandoned or a desire to cut one's parental ties; a desire for security and prestige or the desire for a good mother; a desire to make restitution or the wish to atone for parental sins (for instance, in the event of incest). Such problems may be unconsciously solved by the relationship with God that one expects to achieve by seeking a "vocation." To be sure, these unconscious motives do not ultimately prevent us from being called by God, because God is able to "write straight with crooked lines." Nevertheless, it is beneficial to take a careful look at the effects of these subconscious motives and to complement them with additional reasons for choosing a certain vocation.

In the end, by tracing one's personal story of faith, one can revisit those personal experiences when God was encountered in a *personally beneficial* way. By recalling such life-giving encounters with God we can open the door to different images of the true God that invite us to a personally experienced relationship with him. By repeatedly meditating on positive images of God, such as those described in both the Old and the New Testament, we will become increasingly more aware of the mystery of the true God who faithfully accompanies our lives, constantly sustaining us in continually new ways, especially during difficult times.

Any careful consideration of our images of God can be difficult. Many people simply avoid the subject. We will concentrate here on a few obstacles that experience has shown are frequently encountered during initial consideration of our images of God.

The negative but crucial messages regarding emotions in general, and aggression and anger in particular, that are shared, particularly by people who grew up in a religious home, tend to prompt them to avoid conflict. Examples of such messages are, for instance, that one ought to refrain from showing any emotions, that one ought to keep one's emotions in check, that emotions are bad, even sinful, because they cause human beings to be dependent on their animal drives and desires, that anger must be suppressed, and that any child who wants to be good must not express any anger.

All forms of aggression, regardless of whether they are directed against God or fellow human beings, hold energies that point in a specific direction. If they are not directed at external objects, they are bound to have a destructive internal effect and will be directed against our selves. Anger and annoyance can be suppressed only up to a point before the body will react with psychosomatic illnesses, such as gastritis, angina, asthma, gallstones, kidney stones, high blood pressure, or migraine. These may all be merely symptoms resulting from suppressed anger. Many people view aggression as a negative emotion connected to feelings of fear and guilt. Never mind that the meaning of the word "aggression," which derives from the Latin verb *aggredir*, is initially positive, meaning "to walk up to," "to walk ahead of," "to precede," "to turn to." Aggression, understood in this sense, may serve as a first step toward friendship and love. In a positive sense, aggressions release elemental vital forces directed at progress and the future. Based on this interpretation of the word aggression, we can act aggressively in our encounters with God, that is to say, we can take steps toward him. In this way, we can use our feelings of aggression to approach God and replace our negative images of him with the positive ones offered in the Bible. It is only when aggression is out of control and used destructively against others or ourselves that it turns into a force hostile to life.

Repressed aggression can also result in depression, as well as various forms of addiction. Sometimes suppressed anger lurks behind the mask of the person who is continually smiling, and the overly accommodating person who wishes to do right by everybody. The destructive power of suppressed aggression manifests itself whenever suppressed anger is directed uncontrollably and negatively against innocent people.

There is one image of God that can especially block our positive approach to God: God projected as a "makeshift parent." The makeshift parent is a god invented particularly by unwanted and abused children who project onto this god those characteristics that are missing in their life. These are positive characteristics such as affection, physical closeness, shelter, protection, safety, love, and so forth—in other words, everything their parents have failed to provide them. This image of god as the substitute parent is not only present in children, but in adults, too, who are looking to this "benevolent and loving god" for shelter in their imagination. Although this image of god reflects the biblical image of God, the problem is that it is an image rooted in wishful thinking rather than experience. It is operative primarily when they reach their limits of coping with the cruelty of everyday life. No matter how reassuring it might be to seek refuge in the presence of this god, the effort will be fruitless and even destructive if it ends up leading to a dualistic and schizoid way of life, splitting the world into a good world throughout one's interactions with God and an evil world when dealing with fellow human beings.

This idealization of God is found also among children whose fathers have died during their early childhood years or who have never even known their fathers. Because of the absence of their fathers, these children often cling to God as a powerful and protective figure who lends stability and gives meaning to their lives. Only by dealing with and confronting the frequently glorified and idealized father who caused the child's primordial distrust can this seemingly positive image of God be corrected. As a result of a father's sudden departure through death, the child who is still unable to distinguish, rationally or emotionally, between cause and effect stores the message: "You are not worth my remaining with you"; "I am leaving you because you are not worthy of my love." In order to avoid the pain caused by the loss of their father, children project guilt onto themselves, concluding that they are worthless. Overcome by a sense of worthlessness and submissiveness children justify their father's conduct by suppressing their own feelings of anger, loss, and the pain of abandonment. Thus the father continues to be idealized, remaining great in childrens' imaginations.

It is not easy to remove this idolized father from his lofty perch. Admitting to and directing feelings of hatred, anger, and aggression against him would once again open old wounds and cause renewed pain. This internal, psychological avoidance strategy is underpinned by guiding principles such as: "Never speak badly about people who have died," or "Leave the dead in peace." People who are guided by these or

similarly projected "wished-for father-images of
God" tend to describe their relationship with God
as follows: "I depend on God and could not live
without him. I am holding on to God, clinging to
him, God is the mainstay of my life." When they
physically visualize their relationship with God,
they overwhelmingly come up with the images like
these: grasping for God, throwing their arms
around God's neck, holding onto his knees,
grabbing hold of one of his arms, and so forth. All
the while, God is aloof, allowing all these things to
happen and looking past the person behaving in
this fashion. While those who are reaching out
initially view their relationship as one inspiring
trust and offering protection and as generally
positive, people observing this kind of behavior
view it quite differently, calling it a one-sided
relationship. They suggest those who truly trust
God refrain from grasping and clinging to him.
Instead, they would let go of him. Only then can
they discover that God will not drop them. Instead,
he will catch them in his arms.

But the fearful insist: "You are just fooling
yourself." Little by little, through counseling or
spiritual direction, such misguided people can
come to understand that a very basic form of
distrust is actually hiding beneath their seemingly
positive relationship with God.

Clearly, it will not be easy to take this idealized
god, who has been invented out of necessity, and

unmask him as a makeshift parent. The disappointment that inevitably results will reveal that hidden beneath this seemingly positive image of God is really a negative god who instills fear in us and who threatens us. This is a god we cannot trust and who ultimately will leave and abandon those who cling to him; indeed, this is a demonic image disguised as a positive figure.

At this point, an exercise may be helpful. During retreats focusing on clarifying our actual relationship with God, I have participants act out how an image of God that both instills fear and punishes can interfere with ways of coming to terms with God. This is a modified form suitable for personal use.

Close your eyes. Let yourself become aware of your body and how the floor is supporting you. Now imagine God as a person, for instance a merciful father, who is standing before you with open arms.

How will you respond to God's loving offer to embrace you? Try to express your response with your hands. What position or gesture best expresses your relationship with the divine other?

If any of these gestures expresses your relationship with God, express them now: your hands opened . . . made into a fist . . . used defensively . . . grasping or looking for something . . . your hands covering your eyes, ears, and mouth . . . your hands resting on the midsection of your body . . . or reaching for your heart . . . your hands reaching out toward God. Have you ever wanted to shake your fists at God? Do so now.

Now take a few moments to silently reflect on these gestures and positions with God.

At this point, select one or two gestures or positions that seem especially appropriate to express your relationship with God at this time. Assume this position once again and consider the emotional reactions triggered by it. You may wish to record these in your journal.

As mentioned earlier, one important gesture is shaking one's fists. Most participants find it difficult to shake a fist at God, or worse, to hold that position for any extended period of time. They let their fists drop as if by instinct, open them, or hide them behind their back. Afterward, when they assess their behavior, they utter statements like: "I was afraid"; "Shaking a fist at God is a deadly sin for me"; "God will punish me for shaking a fist at him." Experience shows that, subconsciously, fear is still fairly widespread among believers.

What petty and distorted image of God is at work here? What negative characteristics are being projected onto God? Do we seriously believe that God is incapable of dealing with our aggression or our shaking fists in a healthy manner? Has he not been aware of our anger all along?

The account of Jacob wrestling with God (Gn 32:23-32), the entire Book of Job, the encounter between Jesus and an angry Martha (Lk 10:38-42), or the parable of the Prodigal Son (Lk 15:11-32) all help us find encouragement. They illustrate how God is able to cope with the anger or even hatred directed toward him. In other words, we ought not to hold back, particularly in view of the fact that God already knows our innermost thoughts.

We encounter additional difficulties during our encounter with God when we transfer to God our conflict-ridden relationship with our parents. If our parental ties are very strong, dealing with them aggressively becomes rather difficult. Occasionally, parental conflicts are worked out indirectly and vicariously through God.

Specifically, this happens if the parents portray themselves as weak or as victims, asking for sympathy and help in order to tie their children even more closely to them. Fairly frequently, emotional blackmail is used in statements like: "I have done everything for you"; "You ungrateful son! You call yourself a Christian, but you have abandoned your mother who sacrificed her life for you." This may include even threats and damnations, for instance: "God will punish you for that"; or, conversely, "God will reward you if. . . ."

The consequences of a parent using God as a threat may be that the child reacts in the most extremely negative way. In such instances, children may leave the church or purposely not have their children baptized. They may even become belligerent atheists. Without realizing it, they are reacting to their parents and resorting to the use of religion as a weapon themselves. They are retaliating by using God to hurt their parents' feelings or to punish them for everything their parents have done to them. The degree to which parents and God can be interchanged and confused during this process is illustrated by a young woman in a love-hate relationship with her father. She turned to Jesus on the cross for solace, Jesus whom she deemed weak, instead of confronting her weak father. She referred to her father as a "sissy," but did not dare to confront him directly. Taking a closer look at the image of God she had created for herself, she realized that she had likened God to the Germanic god of war, Odin. One can detect under his helmet the features of her impotent father whom she wished had been strong and powerful. In a poem commenting on the painting entitled "Odin: God of War" she wrote the following:

At the moment the other one,
the pale one,
the gentle God
from Nazareth,
is no longer suffering,
has taken his final breath,
dying,
is lying down in the tomb, strong indeed.
Then it will be your turn . . .
the pregnant world of Calvary,
singed by the breath of death, flares up again,
more frightfully.
Oh, how the fields are expanding
in your morning's radiance.
The ocean is roaring,
echoing you,
muffling your final scream.
On the rood,
my soul is roaring, shouting to you with joy.
Freed by heaven,
I am once again permitted to hate,
to reach for the sword, intoxicated by my
    courage.
The steel is already singing,
whirring through the air.
Horrified, I am breathing the smell
of warm blood.

Here, in the vicarious battle of the gods, this woman's feelings of anger and hatred toward her father are unleashed. To her, the victory of her God, Odin, over the weak Jesus of Nazareth expresses symbolically her victory over her father.

How can we actively engage with God? Once we have acknowledged the presence of a negative image of God, we must take positive and active steps in order to overcome the past. It is dangerous to resign oneself to the repression and self-negation that result from being driven by anger. But at the same time, a more subtle danger exists in trying to move too quickly toward an active engagement with God before anger has run its course. One must go through a time of mourning, which is in fact a form of depression. Unlike mourning, however, anger with God is often directed against oneself. Thus the demonic spirit continues to exert its power. The movement toward an active engagement with God takes place in a series of five steps:

1. As a first step, one should try to articulate the values and the religious orientation of one's parents, their guiding principles. Their images of God should be purposely visualized and examined. This process can be augmented and deepened by other creative methods such as painting, ceramics, sculpting, writing, or physical representations of the images of God.

2. This is followed by examining one's own image of God, which has developed from the images of God advocated by one's parents and by other primary caregivers, or from their religious values and actions. This image of God can be examined using questions such as: Which characteristics

and attitudes have I transferred from my parents to God? Which childhood messages—especially the negative ones—have I subconsciously attributed to God? What negative, demonic image of God was formed in me as a consequence of these messages or of my own negative behavior? Which of these images is now interfering with my life? What survival strategies have I carried over from childhood into my religious life and relationship with God in order to win his recognition and affection?

3. Following this phase of conscious reflection, it will be time to come to engage God more directly. This involves taking a closer look at one's life, beginning with the moment of conception. One should write down all those things God has been expecting since early childhood. These may be negative things that caused suffering and misery and produced psychological injuries and wounds that last a lifetime. They leave great deficits in the areas of affection and love.

This is when the questions and accusations begin: "Where was God during my childhood when I needed him? Why did he keep leaving me in the lurch? Why did he make or, at a minimum, allow all those bad things to happen to me, all those painful experiences I had to endure? Couldn't he have prevented them?" The responses to these questions could be the basis of an angry letter to God. It might start out on a rather cerebral level at first and be fairly unemotional. But one can still tell God about the reasons for anger and blame God for all the disappointments. The letter's message will be more forceful if it is read aloud in the presence of a group of trusted friends, thus making it public. Experience has shown that the accusations will then reach a deeper emotional level and the feelings of anger and anguish can then rise to the surface.

Physical gestures can help support the confrontation of God: making a fist, screaming, throwing stones into the ocean (a symbol of God), beating the surface of the water with one's fists or a stick are all physical ways of expressing anger. During these actions, the other at whom the aggressive behavior is aimed can be recognized more clearly.

During this phase, the psalms can be rephrased to replicate one's anger. Psalm 139 is particularly suited to this purpose. In an angry letter, a fifty-three-year-old woman wrote the following:

> Where were you, you who calls himself the
>   God of the living,
> when my mother rejected me,
> wishing I was dead while I was still in her
>   womb?
> Where were you, you who calls himself "friend
>   of children,"

when I barely escaped death during delivery?
Was it you who wrapped the umbilical cord
    around my neck?
Yes, and what about my childhood?
I was neither wanted nor loved;
I was simply dragged along.
I was miserable, forced to pay dearly for my
    existence
by being on my best behavior, by working
    endless hours:
"Do a good job and you will be respectable;
    this is what God likes."
What were my opportunities,
having a depressive mother and a mostly
    absent father?

You just stood there, watching me.
What joy you derived from my weakened
    existence.
You vampire-god!
How often have I implored you:
"Take my life so that others will have a better
    life."
But all you did was smile at my powerlessness.
I am angry because I fell for your lies.
You lied to me and deceived me.
You took advantage of my childlike beliefs.
You were nothing but an extension of my
    parents
who kept referring to you,
telling me that you loved me,
that you died on the cross for me.
But now I know that you are but a demon.

The true God, the one I am seeking, is a different kind of God.
I can now sense him in the deepest corners of my soul.
He is truly the God in whom I want to place my trust,
the God of life and love,
who has always carried me and who accompanies me even now.
I already sense something of the fullness of life he promised me through my baptism.
Thus I turn to you, the true God of my life.
You will never leave me, in good times or in bad times.
In you I want to put my trust.
Bless me, good God of my life.

4. The difficult phase of active confrontation is commonly followed by an inner liberation. This is frequently connected to experiences of emptiness and deep yearning. Initial suspicions that God is really different from one's childhood image lead to the abandonment of these images, even of those trusted childhood experiences that had been innately positive and good thus far. What matters now is that, in light of the disappointments, one lets go of these images so that one's relationship with God can progress and grow. Letting go is difficult, for on an emotional level God is still a stranger. He acts differently from the way in which he has been experienced up to this point. In

addition, one begins to realize that the God who has been served until now is a demonic god. All these impressions lead to a deep mourning that needs to be acknowledged, expressed in detail, and brought to a conclusion within a reasonable amount of time. A farewell letter to the God of one's childhood can be an additional help. The judicious use of discernment of the spirits will be helpful at this point; for example, in the form of an oral or written dialogue between the good spirit of God and the evil spirit of the demon. This dialogue may quickly reveal that the evil spirit, the negative spirit, tends to pick up on and whisper into our ears those life-denying and negative parental childhood messages: "You cannot do that," "You are not worthy of this," "Life's promises are meant for other people, not for you," "Give up, don't even try." On the other hand, the good spirit gives hope and encourages us to opt for life. He strengthens our self-confidence and he encourages us to use our own individual strengths and vital energies during our search for the true God. This is the time to decide which messages to obey. Following the dialogue between the good and the evil spirit, one selects and formulates personal principles of life. We turn to them, determined to realize them concretely in our everyday lives and in our faith.

Read the angry letter once again after some time has elapsed and observe that the feelings of anger and anguish have slowly become transformed into mourning and a desire for reconciliation and new beginnings. The time has come to compose God's answer to the angry letter. In doing so, we put ourselves in God's place in an attempt to view our own life through his eyes and with his heart.

In most cases, this response letter ushers in a qualitatively new relationship with God, a warm relationship that is clearly distinguished from the frightful and destructive ties to the demonic god.

A forty-five-year-old priest wrote this letter which he called "God's Letter to Me" after wrestling with God for two years:

> *My dear A,*
> *Where are you?*
> *I have been looking for you for quite some time.*
> *I have been longing to throw my arms around you.*
> *So often you were afraid and would run off.*
> *All I wanted to do was to fulfill your deepest wish,*
> *to let you feel how dear you are to me.*
> *I wanted to let you feel how aware I am of your disappointment and your anger.*
> *I even know your pain.*
>
> *Have I not always stood by you,*
> *watching over you and protecting you?*

I have given you warmth and shelter,
when your mother rejected you after she had
    conceived you,
when she had a difficult time accepting you,
I watched over you and your mother
during your life-threatening birth.
How happy I was when everything went well
    for both of you.
I was with you during your miserable and
    loveless childhood.
You were forced to buy affection with
    achievements and accomplishments.
I witnessed your tears,
catching them in my hands,
both the ones you shed and the ones you
    suppressed.
I even added a few of my own, believe me,
for have I not given you life
so that you would be cheerful and happy?
It hurt me to witness
how unfortunate you sometimes were.

Think of the many celebrations of the eucharist
    you attended.
Surely you remember the peace and the sense
    of security I gave you there.
On the day of your first communion, I touched
    you in a special way
when I revealed myself to you.
Through your parish priest my entire
    goodness reached out to you
when the demon of suffering was drawing
    near,

putting his spell on you.
Indeed, you already understood me when you
were still a child,
when I touched your heart.
Through Taizé I was able to let you feel
that I had a personal stake in you through my
Son,
that you are highly valuable to me
and that I have admitted you into my heart,
without asking anything in return from you.

During those times I loved you so dearly
that you became intoxicated and overcome
with emotion.
Do you remember?
And when you accepted me with youthful
enthusiasm
I was happy and felt overwhelmed.
I was always close to you:
during your days in the monastery,
when you were a novice, able to experience
friendship for the first time
and to discover your human side,
during the tough years of studying at the
university
that sometimes brought you to the brink,
but which also allowed you to develop a
healthy sense of self-assurance.
In those days, your very warmth and
excitability
was balm to the souls of many people.
And through your ability to listen, through
your calm and your modesty,

*others recognized me without you ever
    noticing it.
Once again, I was touching you
through the children from the poor sections of
    town
to whom you read from books.
Do you remember how they made friends with
    you,
how they sought your closeness and how they
    wanted to test their strength?
I was so happy about the fatherly feelings they
awakened in you.*

*Dear A, I am not the demon you venerated
    unknowingly for a long time.
No, I am the God who loves you with all his
    heart.
I want to meet you as a freely consenting
    partner.*

In looking back on his experiences of God,
John Henry Cardinal Newman wrote a similar
prayer:

*God looks at you personally, whoever you are,
whatever your condition. He calls you by your
name. He sees you and he understands you
because of the way he created you. He knows
what is inside you, all your feelings and all
your thoughts, your talents and your desires,
your strengths and your weaknesses. He looks
at you on the days you are happy and he sees
you on the days you are in mourning. He feels
your hopes and your tribulations. He takes*

part in your fears and in your memories, when your spirit rises and when it falls. He embraces you and carries you in his arms. From your facial expressions he is able to tell if you are smiling or if you are crying, if you are a picture of health or if illness makes you look sick. He looks tenderly at your hands and your feet. He listens to your voice, to the beat of your heart, even to your breath. There is no way that you love yourself more than he loves you.

5. Following the dismissal of the demonic god and reconciliation with the true God, it is appropriate to remind ourselves of and to write down our personal story of salvation. During that process, the many positive experiences with God that have been covered over by the negative messages of the demonic image of god will become visible. Now, even the seemingly negative experiences will appear in a new light. It is also good to compose a personal prayer of thanksgiving as a testimonial to the blessings and to the love we have received from God.

HEALTHY AND UNHEALTHY IMAGES OF GOD

God is present in all things, yet we are always searching for him. We search above all within ourselves, for we have been created in his image. The divine *ruach*—the Hebrew word for breath, spirit—breathes life into us with every breath we take. God lives within us, even during the painful times in our lives. If this is so, then we, too, can dwell in these painful stories and learn to be at home even with these times of our lives. In this way, our life stories can become stories of salvation despite the presence of hurt.

That is why we must pay attention to both those images of God that can be life-denying and those that are life-affirming. In the remainder of this book we will examine four sets of images. We will look at four demonic images of God and four corresponding healthy images of God that supercede them. The four unhealthy images will be the punitive image of God as judge, the image of God as the personification of death, the image of God as a bookkeeper (which research on counseling and spiritual direction highlight as most prominent), and finally the image of God as a demanding taskmaster. For each of these four demonic images we will examine a healing, liberating image of God gleaned from Christian revelation: the merciful and loving God, the God of life, the Good Shepherd, and the God of fruitfulness.

The process of healing and growth is made more difficult or even prevented by the presence of demonic images of God. These images often disguise themselves, rising out of our subconscious in a way that frequently leads those who are affected by them to believe that they are positive images of God. These demonic images of God can determine one's whole value system—relationships, basic principles, and behavior. They create a vicious circle. Those who are affected by them keep fulfilling their demands. For instance, an achievement-obsessed demon demands more and more success in order to obtain its respect. No matter how much one performs or achieves, it will never be enough. The demands one imposes on oneself grow heavier and heavier until one's strength is completely sapped and all vital energy is exhausted.

This vicious circle can be broken only by a determined effort. We believe in the ultimate victory of Jesus Christ over demonic powers, even though their influence continues in our days and affects our lives. The conscious confrontation of our own unconscious images of God may help us to discern the spirits and to achieve a living and personal relationship with the true God who champions life for us and the world, who affirms and loves us.

This God of revelation is encountered above all through the person of Jesus Christ who became incarnate. Jesus reveals God to us as a loving trinitarian *thou* in the persons of the Father, Son, and Holy Spirit. Jesus dwells in us through the Spirit as a healing force, a source of life and love. Through Jesus, God's fundamental disposition toward all human beings is made visible: respect for the dignity and freedom of each individual, supported by a fundamental affection and love that lasts regardless of whether a person decides for or against God.

The Old and the New Testaments portray the true God as a God who is always for us, who, in the words of St. Augustine, is longing for all human beings. On the one hand, he is the God who lovingly goes out to meet all human beings, like the merciful father in the story of the Prodigal Son. On the other hand, God invites us to assume responsibility for our lives, to work with the talents he has bestowed upon us, and to come to a clear decision for or against him. In the Christian sense, the decision for God is tantamount to a decision for life in its fullness. It includes a healthy love of self, of all human beings, and of God. Therefore we encounter the life-giving images of God above all in the life, the conduct, and the good news of Jesus.

Even the unconscious, demonic images of God point eventually to the positive aspects of God. Thus God as death stirs up fear within us. But as an antagonist of the life promised us by God, he opens our eyes to God as the one who bestows the fullness of life upon us. Similarly, God in the guise of a destructive judge points out laws and rules. But as we live these laws we may discover their true purpose. We may find our direction, we may begin serving the poor or working for justice. The "taskmaster god" who is destructive because of his one-sidedness can alert us to the fact that our achievements and success are truly valuable as long as they are not prized excessively, as long as they serve the kind of fruitfulness that respects human limitations and permits room for creativity. The accountant god whose demonic disposition leads to perfectionism can remind us to refrain from focusing only on ourselves and to pay attention to and have a heart for our fellow human beings. In other words, God in the role of accountant indirectly teaches us that love becomes fruitful through good deeds.

The positive images express both the intimate closeness of God and the inaccessibility of the hidden mystery of God. The following song written by Huub Oosterhuis expresses this quite appropriately:

Lord, our Lord, how present you are,
how unspeakably close you are.
You care for us at all times,
you shelter us in your love.
You are not distant,

and those who pray to you know
that you will never abandon them.
You are so human, living in our midst.
Therefore, you clearly understand our words.
We cannot see you with our eyes—
nobody has ever seen you.
Yet we sense your presence and we know
that you are supporting us, and thus we
perservere.
You are deeply hidden in every living, growing
thing,
yet you wish to dwell in us, human beings.
You devote your entire strength to this effort.
Lord, our Lord, how present you are.
Wherever there are human beings on earth
you are there, benevolent and merciful,
always caring for us,
until we become wholly present in you.

THE DEMONIC JUDGE OR THE GOD OF MERCY AND LOVE?

The Demonic Judge

God as a punitive judge is perhaps at the root of all the other negative images of God. This is a presence that instills fear, one who is a frightening super-god. In his book *The Poisoning of God*, Tilmann Moser, a leading German psychologist, settles accounts with this threatening image of God in the role of judge:

Fear and love God. . . . This was pounded into me as if the first image did not render the second one completely impossible. And because God's irrational presence, as the one who was to be both feared and loved, generated hatred, I was all the more frightened, submissive, humble, and even more grateful, if only to delay God's rejection of me.

This demonic god is described as a pitiless judge who punishes each and every infraction without ever asking for motives or explanations. This tyrant tolerates no contradiction; he knows no mercy, no understanding or kindness. The sinner must do penance and be punished until order is once again restored. No trace of the God of the Old Testament who is a just judge, who sees to it that the weak and suppressed are afforded their rights, remains.

One variation on the image of God as a punitive judge is the strict and omnipotent father-god who rules over his children. Human beings are able to satisfy this great paternal authority only by acting like well-behaved, obedient children. These father-god images are patterned mostly after the paternal model experienced during childhood. As a rule, those who suffered from a negative image of their own father develop problems in their relationship with the father-god. This relationship is characterized by fear and distrust. It may result in slavish obedience, submission to or dependence on authority, and a lack of individual responsibility. Connected to the image of God in the role of judge is a punitive, i.e., retaliatory, animism that insists that God punishes specifically that part of the body that was involved in committing a sin.

There are quite a few people with low self-esteem who try to appease the pitiless judge by punishing themselves in order to avoid condemnation. All that pent-up anger resulting from being unable to live and exist the way they would like to is not directed at God or their fellow human beings, but aggressively against themselves: "Why should I consider myself lovable or my life worth living? Why should I act accordingly if neither God nor other people think that I am lovable or that my life is worth living? If I have messed up my life, why should I go on living?" This kind of thinking comes from the transference of key negative experiences during childhood to one's adult faith life. Along with them comes the feeling of inferiority; these people believe subconsciously that God is not behaving any differently from the way their parents did during their childhood. As to religious matters, they arrange these aspects of their lives in such a way that they will only end up in the same old situation one more time: "I am not lovable and my life is not worth living. Even God only tolerates me." In doing so, they burden themselves with crosses of their own making, and turn even the healing power of suffering against themselves in self-destructive fashion.

The situation becomes destructive when people, who feel the demonic judge breathing down their necks, take refuge in negative asceticism, depriving themselves in a harmful way. They consider such destructive behavior positive and believe that self-negation and humiliation are encouraged by God. In their deep-seated distrust of the pitiless judge who "knows no mercy" and who wants to humiliate and penalize them as sinners, they discipline and castigate themselves, considering this the ransom to be paid for the privilege of being allowed to go on living. They are convinced that this may help them escape the chastisement and the impending punishment of the retaliatory divine judge at the end of their lives.

The price that faith must pay to this demonic image of God is high indeed. Their very existence is haunted, the only way for them to live is under this dark cloud. They are convinced that their lives are worthless and that they cannot attain any measure of self-determination or freely offer any devotion. They are sustained only at the mercy of a despot. Furthermore, they firmly believe that they are no more responsible for their miserable lives than they are for their childhood, since both were dealt to them by an impassive god. Since they see their lives as not worth living, they view themselves as a constant reproach to God who created "such garbage."

Another way of avoiding any confrontation with the dangerous and severe divine judge is to distance oneself from him. By portraying him as a remote God who allows us to live our lives as we please, their angst is suppressed and the might of his threat is thwarted. This is the image of God as an old, decrepit grandfather sporting a long, white beard. Admittedly, it won't take long for the suppressed fears to resurface and for the harmless God whom we had seemingly banished from our presence to reassert his claim.

It is not easy to get people whose faith is mired in fear and trembling to go through a discernment of spirits and to come to terms with their past. Only by consciously working with these problems will they be able to recognize the elements of recurrence and transference in their religious lives and to decide which principles they wish to follow in their everyday conduct.

Ultimately, the destructive vicious circle of self-punishment and denial of one's life can be broken only to the extent that the one-sided pseudo-image of God as a cruel and relentless judge is unmasked as demonic and replaced or augmented by positive images from the scriptures.

The Merciful and Loving God

The demonic image of the punitive, pitiless judge who instills fear and terror is juxtaposed by the image of the true God: the merciful and loving Father who takes care of his children like a Mother. Perhaps the strongest portrayal of this love is in the parable of the Prodigal Son (cf. Lk 15:11-32). Out of his love, this merciful God liberates his children even at the risk of their leaving home, moving to a distant land, and gambling away everything. Yet, he is waiting for them with outstretched arms, not to punish them but to bless them. Lost sons and daughters have already been sufficiently punished for their waywardness and failures. All the father wants them to know is that the love they were searching for in all the wrong places has existed all along, has always been present, and will always be there for them.

Walter Habdank's famous picture of the return of the prodigal son portrays God also as a mother who welcomes the lost child into her lap and into her heart (cf. Is 49:15 ff.). This God— Father and Mother—loves every one of his children in a special way. The hands of the father, resting lovingly and protectively on the son's shoulders, suggest that as long as his son is in need of his protective love he will gladly extend it to him. Yet he has no intention of holding on to him as if he were something to be possessed. The hands of the son, who is resting in the lap of the father, sense the father's heartbeat and love, a love that does not constrain but rather liberates him. All the while, the father looks into the distance, perhaps in the direction of the destination of the life ahead of the son, who will have to make choices following his conversion. Thus, the son will be able to face his destiny with his father backing him all the way.

Against this background, the question is not: How can I find God? But: How can I let God find me? Not: How can I recognize God? But: How can I let God recognize me? Not: How can I love God? But: How can I let myself be loved by God? God is longing for me. Both his paternal and maternal love will never cease. Thus, that very God who had been grieving over his son's departure goes to meet him upon his return and forgives his guilt in advance. All along, the father had known about the hardships his son had encountered, as well as the suffering he had to endure. Love knows no reason why any additional hardships should be inflicted, or why there should be additional suffering or further humiliation. In fact, the pain of love is greater than the pain of guilt. Just as the parable illustrates, God is not interested in our guilt, but rather in our lives. This is God's interest and goal.

Similarly, the father welcomes the son who wants only to work as a day laborer. But the father wishes to bestow the fullness of life on him, symbolized by his festive clothes, his ring, his shoes and, last but not least, the banquet thrown in honor of his son's return. He spares neither trouble nor expense for the returnee; he reconciles with him despite the fact that the son had squandered his inheritance; and he even makes him his heir again. Celebrations and joyfulness are as much part of life as they are part of the kingdom of God where the good news comes to fruition. Be joyful with me, says the father, "'for this son of mine was dead and is alive again; he was lost and is found!' And they began to celebrate" (Lk 15:24). God wishes to share his joy with everybody and that is why he is putting on such a lavish feast.

The ultimate and most profound interpretation of the parable is found when we see Jesus in each character. Jesus is the true son of the father. He is the younger son who never rebels. He is also the older son who refuses to withdraw out of bitterness. He listens to everything the father has to say without becoming his servant. The father never passes judgment on anybody. Instead, he leaves any judgment up to the son. It is comforting to know that Jesus, our friend and brother, is also our judge, already here on earth and at the end of our earthly lives.

Hans Urs von Balthasar reflected on the justice contained in God's judgment. He concludes that hell, which is frequently portrayed against the background of the image of a punitive God, is ultimately superfluous in spite of the scandalous injustices in this world.

This has nothing to do with minimizing injustices, but with the realization that restitution is impossible without reference to God. There will indeed be a day of judgment, and it will be terrible to end up in the hands of the living God (Heb 10:31). It will be terrible because the experience and recognition of God's love will be infinitely painful. Even if we have failed to believe in it, it will be revealed to us at the hour of our judgment. The scales will fall from our eyes and we will realize how little we have believed in that love, how much life we have missed out on, and how much pain we have unnecessarily caused ourselves and others. This means that there is no such thing as eternal damnation for sins committed during our finite existence. Restitution is possible only within the context of a life with God and with the very victims of evil acts. In view of the unspeakable mercy of God the pain is heightened. Yet this suffering is the suffering of human beings who have been saved.

Jesus says: "Be merciful, just as your Father is merciful. Do not judge, and you will not be judged" (Lk 6:36 ff.). Accordingly, Jesus talks about the mercy of God not only with regard to me and my sins which will be forgiven, but also in an effort to invite me to become God-like and to pass on to others the mercy he is showing me. In the practice of this mercy people who have been marginalized, outsiders, the disliked, even our enemies are included. They, too, are sons and daughters of God. This loving mercy is difficult to implement and possible only against the background of experiencing ourselves as sons and daughters of God and of living a life rooted in a loving relationship with God.

THE GOD OF DEATH OR THE GOD OF LIFE?

The God of Death
The "god of death" is another important demonic image of God. As long as he is not unmasked as an evil spirit, this death-dealing demon is able to exercise his destructive influence because he is frequently mistaken for a good spirit.

Prenatal psychological research confirms that fundamental experiences and attitudes toward life are imprinted in the form of engrams while the fetus is still in the womb. In fact, neither positive nor negative experiences are lost during pregnancy. This confirms that long-forgotten insights handed down to us from ancient civilizations, such as India, Egypt, and Greece, are valid. These civilizations believed that even prior to birth an intensive and complex interaction takes place between mother and child in the womb, not merely physiologically, but also psychologically. In its prenatal state, a child is already participating in the emotions of its mother, storing changes in the stimulative patterns of the mother as well as changes produced by periods of tension experienced by her. Thus, feelings of mourning, fear, pain, anger, shame, and guilt are imprinted on the child while still in its mother's womb.

Therefore, if we want to get in touch with the experiences and attitudes that are imprinted in the form of engrams, it is important to ask: Was I wanted or unwanted when I was conceived? Did my life begin with an affirmation (your life is worth living), rejection (your life is not worth living), or ambiguity (your life is worth living, but only providing certain conditions)? It is not unusual for an emotional, subconscious rejection of a child to turn into an affirmation "for God's sake, the child's, the family's, or the Church's."

The following guided exercise can help one get in touch with the deep feeling of being either wanted or unwanted. At the beginning of the exercise, the participants try to imagine the circumstances, the place, the time, and the particulars when their mother realized for the first time that she was pregnant and expecting a child. Then, the exercise focuses more on the mother and her emotional reaction to the following questions: "What was my mother's spontaneous reaction when she realized that I was alive and well in her womb? What words or sentences would most accurately decide her spontaneous emotional response?" Then, the participants are asked to write down the word or the sentence. Afterward, they are invited to act out with their hands their mother's emotional reaction and decide if it was more positive or more negative. Their imaginative reconstruction of their mothers' spontaneous responses are often characterized by shock, fear, and rejection: "That can't be true." "I am ashamed." "Oh my God!" "What will other people say?" "For God's sake!" "No. Not that!" "Why now?" "Why did it have to happen to me?" These initial rejections or denials by the mothers were frequently accompanied by a direct or indirect wish that the child were dead. We are now recognizing that the children in the womb were privy to these reactions. Even if the mother's reaction was only brief and passing, the effect of these death wishes is real, and there can remain a feeling of being caught beneath the legendary sword of Damocles.

Ambivalent experiences in the womb, especially when reinforced after birth, lay the foundation for subconscious negative feelings and a fundamental distrust toward life. People subjected to these experiences often believe that they have no right to live and feel that their existence is threatened for no reason at all. They further interiorize negative expressions such as "rejected," "unwanted," or "unwelcome," to create a corresponding subconscious image of God, i.e., God in the role of a demon of death. Face to face with this demon, the only chance for survival seems to be to close up oneself to everything, to keep quiet and to subject oneself unconditionally to the demon. "Even though I may seem to be happy and alive in the eyes of others with whom I deal every day and at my job," writes a thirty-six-year-old teacher, "inside I feel as if I were in a tomb. My life is like a dance of death on top of a grave." This person selected the following phrase to describe herself, "I wish I were dead."

One reason why the demonic god of death is capable of unleashing existential fear is his unpredictability: one moment he is friendly, the next, disapproving. As a matter of principle, he leaves people in the dark. He holds life by a thread and is ready and willing to sever it at any moment.

The attitude toward life shared by people in the sway of the demonic god of death seems hopeless and desperate: "My life is worthless and meaningless. There is nothing I can do about it even if I want to. All I want is for it to be over soon. The best thing God could do is to destroy everyone and the world, too. The closer I look, the more I find that behind everything that seems to be good there is a lurking evil. And nothing will ever change that" (statement made by a sixty-year-old woman, a town clerk). Many people are desperately looking for a way out, resorting to patterns of compulsive behavior that are supposed to protect them from the demonic god of death. As a result, some people develop a kind of perfectionism that they describe as "life within a protective inviolable sphere, but without any firm footing or a living identity. There is no room for individuality, weaknesses, or personal needs and desires." No matter how perfect, this sphere will remain ultimately lifeless, at the mercy of the demonic god of death. The situation becomes dangerous when people who experience themselves living, as Psalm 23 says, "in the shadow of death," succumb to a destructive mentality of revenge, basing their actions on the motto: It's either kill or be killed.

Experience has shown that those who, even in their mothers' womb, have had to fear for their lives, whose parents had hoped and prayed they would die, were thus "doomed" to living subconsciously in the shadow of death. Some succumb to the fear of death so strongly that they are able to experience life only when it is severely threatened, only when they live on the edge, by taking great risks. In these borderline situations, they experience a desire for life through their fear of dying. In these moments, they cling to the demonic god of death, shaking and trembling with fear yet hoping that he will spare their lives one more time. Frequently, the dreams of people who

SEEK THE FACE OF GOD

were unwanted by their parents reflect this fear of death. They dream of death threats, chase scenes with no escape, graveyard scenes, dark abysses, executions, etc.

How can such a person find the way to a personal relationship with the God of Life? The first step out of this deadly, vicious cycle is to come to terms with the life-denying messages and to consciously decide against death and for the life God has promised us.

In the eyes of a forty-six-year-old nun suffering from anorexia, the decisive step toward a life of her own was the confrontation with the demonic god of death whom she had subconsciously considered to be the true God. Following a heated dialogue between the evil spirit and the good spirit, she rewrote Psalm 139 to reflect her own life. Here are some excerpts:

> *I firmly believe that you are examining me*
> *and that you know the innermost depths of my*
>   *soul.*
> *But knowing this brings me no happiness.*
> *You merely use the knowledge gained from*
>   *examining me*
> *to bring me to heel,*
> *to break my back.*
> *You grab me from behind and from the front*
> *with your death-dealing thoughts.*
> *You doomed me already in my mother's womb*
> *so that the only way I could manage to live*

was as if I were buried alive.
You selected my parents:
An abusive mother who wanted me to
    spontaneously abort myself
so that she would be able to walk away
    unscathed—
she was perverse, sadistic—
and this so-called father of mine
who abused me sexually, undressing me in
    front of others.

Oh, how many times have you deceived and
    disappointed me.
And yet, in my desperation I hung on to you,
because I needed somebody to support me
    when I feared death.
You shamelessly took advantage of me and my
    fears.
You trained me like an animal to be useful in
    the eyes of others,
and to be abused by them.
I grew old believing in you and now,
as my body, my heart, and my mind are aging,
I am getting weaker.
I recognize now that I took the wrong road
for my entire life.
Were you my enemy, perhaps even my mortal
    enemy?
Am I your enemy, perhaps your sacrificial
    lamb?
I am begging, begging, and begging you
    again.

I hear many sounds,
they all call themselves answers.
I have learned to recognize them all,
and slowly now I am even experiencing the
*   desire to live.*
I sense new beginnings.
Are you by my side now, true God,
perhaps even residing in me?
I feel you ever so close in the deepest corners
*   of my soul.*
Yearning for you, my eyes are opened.
I know you are my true God and my good
*   father,*
who has guided me from the very beginning.
You do not dispense death, you give me life.
Help me to believe all this.

Theology teaches us that Christ ultimately redeems and overcomes both evil and death. Yet, as doers of evil and spoilers, the demons keep trying to pull humanity away from the God of Life over to the side of death. From the point of view of pastoral psychology, this means concretely that to accomplish their task, the demons take advantage of the parents' deadly messages, attempting to pull human beings to the side of death and to deprive them of their hope for life.

Even words that do not directly contain death often reveal something of a dowry of death. Thus, words and phrases such as "love child," "my one and only," "my pride and joy," "my life's fulfillment," "the apple of my eye," "daddy's girl," etc., can reveal on the one hand a positive affirmation, yet, on the other, a negative limit. They can be merely a label, or reflect a symbiotic relationship that can make finding one's identity and growing in it more difficult. They can even prevent it entirely, thus keeping one from self-determination, from developing a life of one's own.

Ultimately, believers must be determined to swear off the demon of death in favor of a clear affirmation of life. They must develop a greater belief in God's promises of life. This means, in particular, renouncing the life-denying messages of parents, those messages that the demon of death has appropriated as his own. God's promises and affirmations of life must be formulated so that his personal message of life is expressed and practiced, step by step, every day. One can, for instance, consciously recall during difficult situations that, through baptism, God has promised life. Or, in the evening, one may consciously reflect retrospectively on the positive, life-affirming experiences of the day just passed.

The God of Life

Without being noticed, the demonic god of death affects many people who view life as suffering or a burden, who spend their lives more in the shadow of death than in the brightness of hope. They do so by putting into practice the negative parental messages and by questioning God's promises of life. Nevertheless, those who set out to unmask this demonic god of death will certainly encounter the true God of Life.

Our baptismal vows invited us to renounce evil in order to live in the freedom of the children of God. This life of fullness is promised personally and unmistakably to each child about to be baptized by calling out his or her name, even if the parents do not want the child.

For some people, it takes an entire lifetime to believe in the promises received from God during infant baptism and to incorporate them into their lives. The doubts planted in them by the demonic god of death are sometimes just too strong. It can be very helpful to frame the promise God gave to everybody through baptism as a positive counter-message.

In the Acts of the Apostles, Peter refers to Jesus as the "Author of life" (Acts 3:15) who shows his disciples and all the faithful the way to the true life: "You have made known to me the ways of life; you will make me full of gladness with your presence" (Acts 2:28). Jesus' life originated in God and could not be killed by death. Indeed, it outlasts physical death because Jesus dwells in God's life-giving realm where neither death, nor any other power or force, "nor height, nor depth" can overcome it (Rom 8:39). Jesus has become for us the font of life, the assurance that, by following him beyond our physical deaths, we, too, will be led into never-ending eternal life. He himself is the very way to life, our hope for life in God that can never be lost. By following him and by entering into a personal relationship with the God of life, we are invited to hold every single shadow of our life's story up to the light of God and to let that light touch it. It is only in that moment that we will be able to discern those messages that serve life from those that do not.

In both the Old and the New Testaments, God reveals himself as a God of life who fills human beings with the spirit of life and who thus lets them participate in his divine life. This happens to the degree that human beings allow their lives to be animated by the Spirit of God. Thus our lives are hidden "with Christ in God." When, however, Christ, who is our life, is revealed, then we "also will be revealed with him in glory" (Col 3:3, 4).

In the Old Testament, God's Spirit, *ruach*, is associated with the idea of the wind and the life-giving breath of God. In the beginning, the life-giving *ruach* of God hovers over the waters (Gn 1:2). The Creator breathes his breath into the human being he had formed from clay, thus making a living being out of him (Gn 2:7). We accept this breath and, with it, take part as active participants in the creative act of sustaining life; for it is the breath of the Creator that keeps Adam alive. God's breath of life is able to bring the dead back to life, just as Ezekiel reports in his vision (Ez 37:9). He is also able to revitalize in us all that has been made rigid or killed off by messages of death. However, this life-giving *ruach* is not under our control.

In the New Testament, particularly in the Acts of the Apostles and John, Jesus is proclaimed the fountain and force of life. In contrast to the demon of death, Jesus leads human beings to life, for death was overcome in him. "But God raised him up, having freed him from death, because it was impossible for him to be held in its power" (Acts 2:24). Thus, the resurrection of Jesus from death to life is the assurance to the faithful that following Jesus will also lead to life through and beyond physical death (1 Jn 5:11 ff.).

Our physical death is unquestionably the final reality of this life. Life on earth is only temporary, terminating in our physical deaths. Death is part of life. It proceeds from God and leads us to completion in God. For those who believe in Christ, this limited, temporal life is merely a precursor, a vigil preceding eternal life in the loving company of God. In Christ, the demon of death was overcome and we are now hopeful and confident beyond death. God promised us: "your life is hidden with Christ in God. When Christ who is your life is revealed, then you also will be revealed with him in glory" (Col 3:3–4).

Whenever we encounter suffering and death in our daily lives, our faith in the God of Life is challenged. Whenever we stand at the graves of the departed where their earthly remains are buried, God asks us the same decisive question about life and death that Jesus asked Martha following Lazarus' death: "Do you believe this?" (Jn 11:26). The story began with Martha stating:

> *"Lord, if you had been here, my brother would not have died. But even now I know that God will give you whatever you ask of him." Jesus said to her, "Your brother will rise again." Martha said to him, "I know that he will rise again in the resurrection on the last day." Jesus said to her, "I am the resurrection and the life. Those who believe in me, even though they die, will live, and everyone who lives and believes in me will never die. Do you believe this?" She said to him, "Yes, Lord, I believe . . ." (Jn 11:21ff.).*

Our Christian faith promises us that those who follow Jesus and believe in him will reach eternal life through death. Jesus preceded us to the glory of the Father in order to prepare a place for us.

The following "resurrection exercise" helps us experience faith more fully, in body, spirit, and soul.

> *The exercise begins with standing up. Feel your entire body, your vital energy, your breath. Seek for the dwelling place of your*

very self, the source of your stance in life by moving through your entire body from your feet to the top of your head. Make yourself aware of the presence of God who comes to you with each breath as the breath of life and remains in you. Ask the Holy Spirit to help you make this exercise fruitful. As a sign of your preparedness, reach out for him with open hands.

Then lay down on the floor, assuming a physically cramped position, the position you would have taken as a child when you felt unwanted, rejected, wished you were dead, forgotten, tossed aside, stepped on, worthless, spurned, etc. At this point, it is important to feel, in spite of the physically cramped and painful position, that the floor is supporting you from below, even in this desperate situation, preventing you from falling into a bottomless void. The floor is the hand of God. Desperate and hurting, you now able to entrust yourself to the floor.

Now move from this position to one that expresses your life's greatest pain, the wound of your life. Try to retrace the fears, the pain, the suffering you had to endure as a child in this negative key position of worthlessness, rejection, abuse, etc. This position has been stored in your body and your body still remembers it.

But do not get lost in this pain. Rather, through all this pain, direct your attention to yearning for liberation and redemption. Feel that yearning in your body's limbs. Try to recall the baptism through which God called you by your name, unmistakably promising you a life of plenty through the symbols of light, water, and oil. In this way, touch God with your neediness. Listen to his promises: "You shall live; I have redeemed you and called you back to a resurrected life. I tell you, get up for I have given you the strength to do so. For I am the resurrection and the life."

At the time of your baptism, your godparents renounced evil, the demon of death, in your name. Now, completely aware of this demonic idol, personally renounce evil once more. Allow the energy and the forces set free in your body by God's promise and by your denunciation of evil to flow. At the same time, recall the positive words with which God addresses you (for instance, precious instead of worthless; accepted instead of rejected).

Out of this trust and belief in God's promise respond, step by step, with your entire body by undoing your captive state and your body's cramped position induced by the negative position. Slowly rise, little by little, and experience how new life is awakened as a result of these movements. Finally, after five to ten minutes, stand up straight and feel resurrected. Return to your original place, assuming your original position. Trace the expanse of your vital energy, as it flows through you and revitalizes your body. Consciously inhale and exhale, feel your life pulsating through your

*body, from your feet to the top of your head;
then rest your hands in your lap.*

*Remain standing for several minutes.
Consciously connect your present situation to
God, feeling how God lives in your breath, and
inundates you. Out of gratitude for having
been redeemed and liberated, conclude this
exercise now by moving around freely, per-
forming perhaps a dance of resurrection with
which you can praise God and give thanks.*

Experience bears out the benefits of repeating
this resurrection exercise daily over a long period
of time until one's body recalls more and more the
upward movement and the continually renewed
sensation of vitality. In this way, it is possible to
slowly discover the path to believing in the
resurrection of life on the physical, emotional, and
mental level, and to allow this belief to take root in
your vital experiences. Admittedly, the wounded
position will continue to exist subliminally in our
daily lives, will continue to interfere. Yet it will lose
its sting as a result of its confrontation with the
individual message of life: "I am allowed to live, I
am alive, and I want to live."

In the story of the revival of Jairus' daughter,
Jesus said to her: *"Talitha, kum"* (Mk 5:41), which
means, "Little girl, get up." These words can help
us understand more deeply the mystery of death
and resurrection. Jesus overcame death and
leads us from death to life. Just like the little girl,

he awakens us to life from the sleep of death with the words: *"Talitha, kum,"* for his love is stronger than death.

THE ACCOUNTANT OR THE GOOD SHEPHERD?

God the Accountant

The "accountant god" is described as a threatening watchdog, a kind of big brother who is always watching us, a painstaking legalist, a sinister snoop, a moralistic overseer, the world's policeman, a loan shark, etc. Almost everybody views this divine accountant as a relentless judge who metes out punishment for recorded misdeeds and sins.

The idea that God's eye notices everything, even things that happen in the middle of the night, is interpreted largely negatively. This image creates distrust making it difficult for people to accept the positive aspects of biblical revelation, e.g., that those over whom the eye of the Lord watches are blessed and fortunate (c.f. Ps 33:18; Job 36:7). God's eye is frequently viewed as threatening and controlling because the true God was abused by parents when teaching their children about religion: "Time and again, my mother would tell me that God sees everything, hears everything, and knows everything about our innermost thoughts." "Even if nobody ever finds out about your sins, God is aware of them and will punish you for them." Thus parents instill in their children a fear of committing sins, sometimes even causing them to be excessively scrupulous. In the eyes of people raised in this fashion, being a Christian means being a slave to an incalculable array of dos and don'ts. They will never be able to obey entirely. It's as if there was a proverbial ledger listing only unpaid bills: disobedience, broken rules, violated laws, or undue liberties. These failings will cause feelings of deep guilt which must be forgiven. But their lives become an ongoing torture because they realize their inability to obey all these laws and rules.

Rules and laws no longer serve as guideposts or aids to a successful life. Rather, they turn into autonomous control mechanisms that keep pronouncing people guilty and passing judgment on them in the name of God. In this negative light, even the psalms will take on a threatening character, as was illustrated earlier with Psalm 139.

Even those who are trained in psychology can experience torment and fear of an omnipresent accountant god. Tilmann Moser summarized his childhood feelings in the following way:

Do you know what the worst trait they told me about you was? It was the mean and insidious

*way in which they tried to convince me that
you hear and see everything, that you can even
hear my most secret thought. From my childhood perspective, I was miserable. I felt like
you were always watching me, mercilessly,
without respite. You were always listening,
amusing yourself by reading my mind. . . .
From my youngest days I was haunted by the
question, "What will God have to say about
that?" I was at the mercy of my guilt.*

This accountant god has shaped entire
generations of Christians: laity, religious and
priests, men and women, even theologians. The
following example may be representative of the
many victims of the accountant god: A fifty-one-
year-old member of a religious order was looking
for a treatment facility for his dependency on
alcohol and prescription drugs, a place where he
could also receive counseling about spiritual
questions. His present therapist had recognized
that some of the issues he was working on related
to religious problems as well as physiological and
psychological ones. The priest was rather
depressed and desperate and told the therapist his
life's story during the first couple of sessions. As a
child of older parents, he was told repeatedly by
his mother that he was an unwanted child, "an
accident because we hadn't been sufficiently
careful." Both the pregnancy and the delivery
were difficult for his mother who was forty-four at

the time. Following his birth, she had to spend several months in the hospital and subsequently suffered a facial paralysis that she considered highly disfiguring. Furthermore, during the pregnancy, she repeatedly was teased by her neighbors who were snickering and expressing their surprise "that somebody her age would still have sexual needs and could even get pregnant." Thus, his mother was ashamed and dressed in ways that did not show that she was pregnant. It was then that she promised God: "If it's a boy, he will be completely yours."

While working on this key issue, the priest recognized that being dedicated to God while still in his mother's womb was his mother's way of atoning for a sex life that she assumed was unbefitting her Christian surroundings and its rules of decorum. "The purpose of sexuality is to produce children." In order to escape God's punishment, she sacrificed her son by "dedicating him to God." This was her way of "getting rid of him." Thus, he could no longer remind her of her sin, and she was now able to give birth to him with a clear conscience. In looking back, the priest interpreted his dedication to God as a "piously disguised form of abortion." He opined that his mother must have wanted him dead repeatedly during her pregnancy and that the best thing that could have happened to her was to get rid of him. The father, who was a devout farmer, asked:

"Honey, how could this have happened?" But then he changed his mind, saying: "Don't be upset. Let's just accept this child as a gift of God."

During his early childhood, the priest was exposed to a variety of conflicting emotions directed toward him by his mother, ranging from affection to rejection. The result was that he felt very insecure. On the one hand, she showered him with tenderness, spoiled him rotten, perhaps because of her feelings of guilt. On the other hand, she was firm, raising him as a well-adjusted, well-behaved boy who was eventually to become a priest.

One day, his mother surprised him and caught him playing with himself under his blanket, apparently enjoying it. He received a sound thrashing and, from then on, had to sleep with his hands on top of his blanket so that it wouldn't happen again, "because God sees everything and writes it down in his sacred book. Woe to you, if you die after committing a mortal sin. You won't be able to stand before God, you'll be sent straight to hell." Soon he became increasingly timid and unsure of himself. This insecurity was exacerbated by a family tradition in which children's good and bad deeds were assessed by either golden or black points each day. These were then written down and added up at the end of the year. Woe him, if he, the future priest, did not end up as the most well-behaved among the children.

At the age of ten, he entered a religious boarding school. Then, after completing prep school he entered the novitiate of a religious order. At the age of twenty-seven he was ordained, much to the pride and joy of his entire family. When he took over a parish at the age of thirty-four, the first psychosomatic disturbances surfaced. He began to stutter while delivering sermons. It took great effort to say the words of consecration. Besides his stuttering, he was afraid of rendering Mass invalid because of any mortal sins he may have previously committed. In addition, he was afraid of dying suddenly after committing a mortal sin while celebrating Mass. He also suffered from panic attacks that he might commit additional mortal sins like the ones mentioned in the headings of books on moral theology. After a while, he began to wash his hands compulsively, a behavior which bothered him greatly. Finally, he could no longer tolerate life without the aid of alcohol and, later, pills. Thus his life became literally wretched. Although he tried repeatedly to rehabilitate himself, he finally relinquished the parish and assumed a less responsible position in a monastery. Yet no matter how hard he tried, his addiction did not get any better.

He felt more and more abandoned by God and believed he was, as he put it, "being rightfully punished for my sins." In particular his inability to stop masturbating, whether despite or because of his many confessions, caused him a lot of pain. In his eyes, "it was and remained a mortal sin, regardless of what liberal theologians kept saying about it." It took a long and arduous effort to finally recognize the real causes behind his sickness and his confusion. In a group therapy session, he described his subconscious demonic image of God as that of an accountant who kept pointing at the demands he had not met and the mortal sins he had committed with an unforgiving finger. Only gradually did he manage to learn to distinguish between genuine and false feelings of guilt.

This example illustrates that, through their fears and feelings of guilt, people who are haunted by their internalized demonic accountant god remain surrounded and tormented by their parental idols and are incapable of discovering a life of their own. Without consciously confronting their past, they remain prisoners of the fears and guilt feelings of their childhood, transferring them to God without even noticing it. Many people who are vexed by a demonic accountant god, a god who is a relentless judge, are liberated by reading about Jesus' encounter with the woman who was a sinner (Lk 7:36 ff.), or his meeting with the adulteress (Jn 8:1 ff.). Likewise, reading about the merciful father in the parable of the Prodigal Son (Lk 15:11 ff.), or the parable of the Good Shepherd (Jn 10, Ps 23). All of these are helpful in gradually drawing them closer to the benevolent and kind God and to helping them believe in his forgiveness.

God as Good Shepherd

If we are searching for an image of God that is capable not only of freeing us from the grip of the accountant god, but of replacing it, we can turn to the revealed image of God as a Good Shepherd who looks after us and cares for us, his sheep. The relationship between the shepherd and his sheep is a most ancient symbol of the caring, tender, protective, and loving relationship between God and human beings. Lambs and sheep are defenseless and easily get lost. They need a shepherd to lead them to secure pastures, to protect them from danger, to search for them when they are lost or have taken the wrong path and to carry them safely back on his shoulders.

This intimate and trusting relationship between sheep and shepherd is described in Psalm 23:

The LORD is my shepherd, I shall not want.
He makes me lie down in green pastures;
he leads me beside still waters;
he restores my soul.
He leads me in right paths for his name's sake.

Even though I walk through the darkest valley,
I fear no evil;
for you are with me;
your rod and your staff—they comfort me.

HEALTHY AND UNHEALTHY IMAGES OF GOD

You prepare a table before me in the presence
  of my enemies;
you anoint my head with oil;
my cup overflows.
Surely goodness and mercy shall follow me
  all the days of my life,
and I shall dwell in the house of the LORD
my whole life long.

In the Old Testament, God constantly accompanies us, preparing the way for his people. He is dependable, especially in difficult situations: "It is the Lord who goes before you. He will be with you; he will not fail you or forsake you. Do not fear or be dismayed" (Dt 31:8).

For instance, Yahweh, the mighty one and Good Shepherd, leads his people out of the Babylonian captivity: "He will feed his flock like a shepherd; he will gather the lambs in his arms, and carry them in his bosom, and gently lead the mother sheep" (Is 40:11). The Good Shepherd keeps an eye on each person; he loves them and makes certain that none of them will get lost. On the other hand, the accountant god watches over the errors and failures of human beings like a hawk, never taking his eyes off them, always controlling them without any consideration for their well-being. The Good Shepherd has a highly personal relationship with every human being: "I am the good shepherd. I know my own and my own know me" (Jn 10:14). The Good Shepherd looks lovingly and thoughtfully at his people. He watches over their well-being night and day. He never takes his eyes off of them lest they might lose their way and come to harm (Ez 34:12 ff.). He makes sure that they are treated justly, particularly standing up for the disadvantaged and the weak (Ez 34:16 ff.).

John's gospel takes up the metaphor of the Good Shepherd, describing Jesus as the Good Shepherd who protects his sheep and who gives his life for them (Jn 10:11). Out of pastoral concern, Jesus puts the false shepherds, the hired hands, on trial for running away at the sight of the wolf. They do not care about the safety of the sheep; all they wish to do is exploit and use them for their own purposes.

Indeed, the accountant god can be easily detected posing as a false shepherd. Jesus does not keep his fold together by using force, by controlling them, or by instilling fear in them. His pastoral concern is characterized by his benevolence and by his close and loving relationship with his fold. The Good Shepherd calls his sheep "by name" (Jn 10:3), talking to them one on one, and they follow him.

The accountant god, too, talks to his sheep individually, trying to get them to join his side. What matters is the difference between the spirit with which the demonic god motivates people and gets them to act, and the spirit with which the Good Shepherd addresses his sheep. The demon is after personal and selfish gain, whereas the Good Shepherd is concerned about the life and the well-being of his sheep. Because he is a good shepherd, Jesus follows the tracks of the lost sheep and rejoices with the entire fold when he has found it again. He does not rest until all his sheep have attained their goal, i.e., eternal life.

Unlike the demonic accountant god, the Good Shepherd ignores the mistakes of his sheep; he does not blackmail them with their weaknesses and their guilt. The Good Shepherd rather frees the sheep from their entanglement in evil.

Thus, a new quality of life emerges. All that the demonic accountant god has recorded in his ledger is now being redeemed by the true God, the true shepherd, the very lamb of God. We can reach this full mystery of life into which the Good Shepherd wants to lead us only if we gradually unmask the accountant god as a false shepherd, erasing his unjustified guilty verdict. Now the sheep will no longer need to go hungry or be thirsty. Now they can live peacefully and live in loving community with God and their fellow human beings. None will be lost because everybody is safe in the presence of the Good Shepherd.

Thus we can put our trust in the Good Shepherd who is benevolently watching over his fold. He sacrificed his life for his sheep so that we will be saved by his death and by his resurrection and thus attain eternal life. He inscribed our names into his hand; in him we will find our safe haven.

God,
I am looking for a hand
that will hold and encourage me,
that will calm and protect me.
I am groping about for a hand
that will accompany and lead me,
for a hand that will heal and save me.
I need a hand
that is strong and carries me,
a hand that reaches out for me and will not let
    go.
I would like to be held by a hand that means
    well,
a hand that gently cradles me.
I am yearning for a hand
that I can completely trust,
a hand that faithfully loves me.
I am looking for a large hand
in which I can rest my little hand,
and my heart as well,
a hand in which I am safe—completely.
God, your hand is inviting me:
Come.
Your hand's presence tells me
that I need not fear.
Your hand assures me
that you love me.
                    —Theo Schmidkonz

THE TASKMASTER OR THE GOD OF FRUITFULNESS?

The Taskmaster God

The "taskmaster god" persuades human beings to overdo an act that is essentially good because, in his eyes, achievement alone matters. The demonic dimension of this seemingly positive image comes to light through its excessive demands. For the taskmaster god, achievement is more important than the abilities or limitations of the people charged with achieving. Even the overachiever who is often convinced that he is doing God's bidding by accomplishing a feat beyond any reasonable expectation, is destroyed by the conviction that it is never enough. The *diabolos*—the Greek word for a person who confuses—may not seduce such a person to do evil, but succeeds by encouraging him to do excessive good.

When asked about the most important principles their parents handed on to them, many people respond by highlighting the importance of things such as the following: "If you accomplish something people will look up to you." "Work sweetens life." "Working hard is the best medicine." "Achievements and success add to a person's worth." Thus, entire generations have been taught to base their self-esteem on achievements and success. They have come to believe that their value as human beings is determined by this.

People who have been raised to fulfill this pattern of achievement and success and who were punished if they did not live up to it have paid dearly for the parental recognition and admiration they received in return. They are often plagued by scruples, perfectionism, compulsive behavior, and existential fear.

Independence and autonomy are particularly threatened. Basic trust is eroded when a mother describes her affection and so-called love as a performance, demanding her children's lifelong gratitude for everything she has done for the them. Often the commandment: "Honor your father and your mother . . . so that your days may be long and that it may go well with you" (Dt 5:16) is invoked. Many people suffer from serious guilt feelings because they rebelled against this symbiosis of presumptive gratitude and guilt by claiming the right to a life of their own. What is striking about families with several children is the relatively large number of first-borns who find themselves in this performance and success-oriented survival strategy. They had to act like adults early on, assuming responsibilities for their younger siblings. They had to work and thus actually earn their parents' respect for their own sense of existential justification.

A childhood determined by an emphasis on achievement is experienced all the more painfully by the first-born because they had enjoyed the attention and benefits of being an only child before another sister or brother was born, taking his or her place. People who were raised to be achievers and whose goals were oriented toward meeting certain standards of performance or even surpassing them expect others to do the same. They frequently transfer onto God these same modes of thinking and experience. They assume that God's love, too, must be earned through individual achievement and as a result of painstaking efforts. Correspondingly, they develop subconscious images of a performance-oriented god who keeps asking for ever greater achievements. Or they may live like parasites dependent on others for approval.

In written accounts about their lives, in imaginative exercises, in dreams and throughout creative exercises, the taskmaster god is portrayed as an ogre whose voraciousness can never be sated. A fifty-year-old nun writes: "Having persuaded people to serve him out of love, this exploitative God abuses them shamelessly. One can never satisfy him; he keeps asking for more." Others characterize this taskmaster god as a bloodsucker. Like a vampire, he drains the vital energy from his victims after making them dependent and addicted to him. He "pretends to

SEEK THE FACE OF GOD

be close to them and fond of them, but changes them into vampires too, who suck the blood of others or even their own."

A despot sitting on a throne is frequently the favorite portrayal of the achievement-demanding, performance-oriented god. This anti-god ignores the needs of human beings until they lay a suitable achievement at his feet. It is at this point that he briefly acknowledges their presence by looking them in the eye or by touching them. He honors them only momentarily, for as long as it takes them to present their achievement. Then he looks past them once again. The gesture of recognition lasts only as long as the presentation of the achievement.

Part of this experience is the realization that God indeed does acknowledge them and turns to them. But the acknowledgment of the achievement is confused with the acknowledgment of the individual. Self-esteem is strengthened temporarily on account of the achievement rendered. But to please this taskmaster, entire dimensions of what it means to be human are bracketed out: the limits of one's ability to perform, weaknesses, illness, all those circumstances that one must overcome to accomplish something have to be simply ignored. Thus, this vicious circle, consisting of achievement and acknowledgment, fails to produce genuine self-esteem. Caught up in this circle, human beings remain externally determined, dependent on the affection of a performance-oriented god or the approval of others. Life seems like a treadmill.

A common variation of the theme of achievement and success is a kind of spiritual activism that is often confused with love for one's neighbor. It is widely practiced within the church and causes a lot of harm. Many priests and pastoral ministers end up suffering from burnout and internal emptiness because they are forced to achieve ever more.

Unmasking the achievement-demanding god turns out to be rather difficult. A misinformed Christian pedagogy in families, Catholic schools, religious education programs, and even in novitiates and seminaries idealizes self-sacrifice one-sidedly. It renders selfless love of one's neighbor absolute and extols it as the greatest of virtues. Hence the maxim: "Love your neighbor above all, but not yourself." This misrepresentation of the second great commandment, "You shall love your neighbor as yourself," stems from one-sided religious upbringing. It is an upbringing based on a selflessness that aims to appease the achievement-demanding God. It overlooks that fact that the only human beings capable of being selfless are those whose self does indeed exist. It is here that the achievement-demanding demon acts like one who destroys the self, doing mischief under the guise of charity and frequently by appearing virtuous. Narcissistic and individualistic tendencies toward self-realization are the consequence of such religiously restrictive upbringing, whose one-sidedness reacts to the lost balance between love of self, love of neighbor, and love of God.

The first step away from this vicious cycle of achievement and excessive demands is the conscious confrontation with the demonic achievement-demanding god who has been influencing and pigeonholing one's life, sometimes even in ways that go unnoticed. The confrontation begins when one decides individually and responsibly which achievement-oriented messages one will take on and which ones one will reject. Ultimately, one reaches a point when priorities consciously change. Some are emphasized, others are not. For instance, if the parental message is, "We live in order to work," one will initially have to reject this message: "No. Work is important, but there's more to life than work. I want to have time for leisure, relationships, and creativity in my life."

The basis for a reorientation of the way we view achievement is the incorporation of human possibilities and limitations. This is an orderly self-love. In addition to periods of work, it also includes quiet times and leisure, the perception of one's individual needs and desires, and the development of one's creativity. It is only in this way that emotions that have been previously missed can be cultivated and the heart's desires fostered. Such an orderly self-love can be practiced by taking little steps such as rejoicing over successes and achievements without allowing this self-love to be dependent upon it.

The stronger orderly self-love becomes, the greater the reach and genuine character of the love for one's neighbor. At the same time, God's love becomes part of the picture, too.

There are many events and parables in the New Testament that can encourage us in this effort: in Jesus' meeting with Mary and Martha (Lk 10:38 ff.), the parable of the Workers in the Vineyard (Mt 20:1 ff.), the parable of the Prodigal Son (Lk 15:11 ff.), or the story of the Pharisee and the Tax Collector (Lk 18:9 ff.). The messages contained in these parables tell us that Jesus does not primarily look for achievement and that his affection is not dependent on it. On the contrary, he takes particular care of the weak, of outsiders, and of those who have been marginalized by society— people who do not possess sufficient strength to succeed or who do not dare to rely on it. Jesus proclaims God as the loving Good Shepherd who rejoices more over the lost sheep he has found again than "the ninety-nine that never went astray" (Mt 18:13). At the same time, Jesus cautions us to refrain from burying the talents God has given us, but to use them instead, regardless of how unique they may be (Mt 25:14 ff.).

The discernment of spirits will be essential if we are to achieve a healthy attitude. The eighteenth-century Jesuit writer Gabriel Hevenesi expressed it in this way:

> Let your trust in God be the primary rule in
>   every activity.
> Act as if every success
> depended completely on you and not on God.
> However, devote all your efforts toward it
> as if you did nothing,
> but God alone achieved everything.

The god who demands excessive achievement can be unmasked only with the greatest of difficulty because he provides welcome support for our modern success-oriented society whose stated and paid goal is, indeed, performance. Of course, it goes without saying that achievement ought to be part of the life of every individual human being because that is the purpose of having energy and talents. But the scriptures invite us to use them with a different goal in mind: Will the achievement benefit the lives of people, of those who are the achievers as well as those who are the beneficiaries of it? Or will it be a hindrance to them?

The God of Fruitfulness

Achievement is not an end in and of itself. Fruitfulness, however, does represent the aim of

Jesus' mission as well as the aim of those who follow him: "You did not choose me but I chose you. And I appointed you to go and bear fruit, fruit that will last" (Jn 15:16), he reminds us. Only the God of fruitfulness can restrain the demanding taskmaster god and at the same time help us clarify what is truly essential.

Jesus' concept of fruitfulness includes human cooperation with God as well as achievement, but Jesus recognizes that God allows events to unfold and grow according to their own timeline. Time and again, he described the kingdom of God using images and parables of fruitfulness: the mustard seed (Mt 13:31 ff.), the weeds growing among the wheat (Mt 13:24 ff.), the seeds falling on the path (Mt 13:3 ff.), the vine and its branches (Jn 15:1 ff.).

This contradicts the values and ideals of our performance-oriented society in many ways. Society says the worth of every individual is determined by the degree and the nature of his or her achievements. Everything must be earned, including affection, gratitude, respect, and love. "I don't deserve all this love," we hear people say. Or, "He has to earn respect; he has not accomplished anything worth crowing about yet."

A lot of people complain about how much work they have to do and their numerous appointments and phone calls. Yet they wouldn't want it to be any other way because they define themselves by the amount of work they do. Saying that we don't have time has become a status symbol, a badge of distinction rather than a flaw. The achievement-demanding demon hidden beneath these claims does not even spare older people who sometimes complain that they have even less free time now than they did when they were working.

While the fact that fruitfulness includes achievement can sometimes blur the line between them, there are essential differences between the taskmaster god and the God of fruitfulness. The achievement-demanding demon wants to know everything, determine everything, and control everything with only one goal in mind: ever greater production. Indeed, only the highest degree of achievement will do. The achievement-demanding demon is interested only in the actual accomplishments and ignores the human being who is responsible for them. He could not care less about how the achievement was accomplished or what its effect might be on the achiever. By contrast, the God of fruitfulness encourages growth. He provides the seed; we plant it so that it can grow. Growth takes place secretly without much influence by human beings. The fruitfulness itself leaves room for the mystery.

To acknowledge the God of fruitfulness requires us to be patient and allow growth to take place. Jesus describes this growth in the following parable of the Seed Growing by Itself:

"The kingdom of God is as if someone would scatter seed on the ground, and would sleep and rise night and day, and the seed would sprout and grow, he does not know how. The earth produces of itself, first the stalk, then the head, then the full grain in the head. But when the grain is ripe, at once he goes in with his sickle, because the harvest has come" (Mk 4:26-29).

Here the achievement-demanding demon who wants to teach us how to dominate everything meets his match. While we can either promote or prevent growth, real growth and fruitfulness lie in God's hands. The same is true with other fundamental human values like friendship, love, happiness, and health. We can receive them, accepting them as gifts; we can let them grow and promote them, or we can work against them. But ultimately they are not under our control. Those who allow themselves to be dictated by the taskmaster god, those who seek success for its own sake, will end up empty-handed when they can no longer be sufficiently successful on their own. What will they be worth then? Our achievement-oriented society rewards those who are successful and work their way up the corporate ladder. But it shows no mercy to those who fail, who produce less, who are weak and sick, who are getting older, or who simply pursue goals that differ from the ratcheting up of one's performance. It is here that the God of fruitfulness tells them:

> *You need not make the impossible possible.*
> *You need not live beyond your possibilities.*
> *You need not fear.*
> *You need not do everything.*
> *You need not perform miracles.*
> *You need not be ashamed of yourself.*
> *You need not meet every demand.*
> *You need not meet every expectation put to you.*
> *You need not play a role.*
> *You don't always have to be strong.*
> *You don't have to go it alone.*
> —*Andrea Schwarz*

As illustrated by the story of creation, the God of fruitfulness pays attention to the laws of nature and the dignity of human beings (Gn 1:11). The taskmaster god, however, shows no consideration for nature or human beings. In recent decades, we have experienced the extent of nature's exploitation at the hands of our performance-oriented society and the consequences of this exploitation in various environmental crises and catastrophes.

People, too, are ruined by excessive pre-occupation with business and the attempt to fulfill extraordinary demands. Burnout is merely one outcome of this abuse. An achievement-oriented, active lifestyle is indeed a vicious cycle. The emphasis on achievement destroys relationships and has a negative influence on the family and society. Its objective is to make certain that each of us is always striving to be better than the other. When achievement is our highest goal, competition and rivalry mar our relationships. There is constant comparison of winners and losers. Ultimately, this self-centered emphasis on success and achievement affects our relationship with God. For the true God does not look first for achievement. Rather, he looks at the human being. In this encounter with the true God of fruitfulness, the achievement-demanding demon loses his power. We are challenged to reverse our course.

The God of fruitfulness permits weeds to grow among the wheat until harvest time (Mt 13:24–30). There is profound wisdom in allowing the weeds to grow. People who are perfectionists, striving incessantly to achieve flawless excellence, pose a great danger both to themselves and to others. The history of the church throughout the ages and in our times bears witness to numerous examples of acts of fanaticism and cruelty perpetrated in the name of a perfectionist god. The God of fruitfulness takes the weaknesses and sins of human beings into account. He accepts us just the way we are and not how we are expected to be according to the plans of the achievement-demanding demon: strong and powerful, without blemish, without any wounds or weaknesses. The New Testament teaches us that grace shows its greatest strength when we are weak (2 Cor 12:9).

Those who obey the taskmaster god run the risk of filling times of prayer, leisure, or recuperation with achievements. In 1145, Abbot Bernard of Clairvaux warned his former confrere, Pope Eugene III, about the achievement-demanding demon in a letter that still applies today:

> *I am constantly worried about you. . . . I am afraid . . . that, hemmed in by your numerous activities, you no longer see a way out of our predicament and that you have therefore become hard-hearted. . . . It would be much more prudent to walk away from your activities from time to time instead of allowing them to push you in a direction you don't want to go . . . to a place where your heart will harden. To briefly sum up all the evils of this terrible illness: When the heart hardens both our fear of God and our feelings for our fellow human beings are lost (Lk 18:4).*
>
> *Look, this is where your confounded activities are taking you. You are wasting your time . . . and you are senselessly wasting your energy on them. The result will be that your spirit will suffer, your heart will be hollowed out, and grace will disappear into thin air. Tell me, what are the fruits of all these activities? Aren't they but mere spider webs?*

The God of fruitfulness introduces a contemplative dimension into the life of human beings. This dimension requires time to envision the existence of things and time in order to be able to see through them all the way to the center of the mystery that dwells within everything. Admittedly, it is not easy to stop and reflect. Contemplation challenges us to a deeper encounter with self as well as careful self-examination. Yet only if we know ourselves can we know God and become contemplative. This will affect the way in which we perform our work: contemplative people perform their duties and work with the same degree of transparency toward God as they have when they pray. What matters is not *what* we do but *why* and *how* we do it. This is particularly illustrated by the parable of the Grain of Wheat in which Jesus proclaims the fundamental law of all fruitfulness in the kingdom of God: "Very truly, I tell you, unless a grain of wheat falls into the earth and dies, it remains just a single grain; but if it dies, it bears much fruit" (Jn 12:24). The very mystery of fruitfulness is discovered when we perform our activities with a willingness to allow things to happen and with an acceptance of them coming from God. Ultimately, this amounts to a dying, and it is the basis on which new life will constitute itself.

St. Paul frequently points out a similar problem: our salvation is not accomplished by the law, but by our faith. When we take as our own the maxim "we are what we do," our lives are rendered absurd in the arena of faith. We are not able to earn our salvation by obedience to the law. We cannot force God to give us our reward. People who think and live this way are subjecting themselves to the achievement-demanding demon.

As we get older, our so-called achievements become diminished in the eyes of the world. This becomes apparent relatively early in the lives of professional athletes when both their bodies and spirits begin to lag. In view of these realities, the achievement-demanding demon jumps on a new opportunity: he confronts older people with standards of performance and youthfulness that they cannot possibly live up to, no matter how hard they try. The same applies to people who are physically and mentally challenged who are unable to perform "normally," but who keep using normality as a standard for themselves, thus attempting the impossible. The God of fruitfulness sets up a different standard, the one described in the Sermon on the Mount. Everyone possesses unique, special talents and possibilities, everyone also has the power to fulfill this potential. At this point, our fundamental Christian attitude takes shape: God has freely given us everything and he will neither tempt us nor put demands on us that will exceed our capabilities.

I thank you, Lord, for the gift of freedom.
You created me as a free human being
and you destined me to share
my freedom with all the sons and daughters of
    God.
Now you are creating me anew,
again as a free human being.
I am no longer what I was.
I am no longer only what I have made of
    myself,
but what you have made of me.
You do not ask me to perform.
You do not judge me on my failures.
I am yours.

Once I was a captive, but now I am free.
I am baptized in your name.
I am your child and will always be.
Newly created by your Spirit,
the creator Spirit,
I will no longer ask if I deserve to live,
for I live now through you.
I thank you, Lord,
now and in all eternity.

—Jörg Zink

CHAPTER FIVE

A CONFESSION OF FAITH

*God, I believe that you are completely different
from the way I imagine you,
that you can never be described
in words or image.*

*I believe in you, sacred force,
who are both Mother and Father to us.
In your wisdom and goodness
do not let suffering and neediness separate us
from you.*

*I believe that you created both the heavens and
the earth,
the universe with its solar and planetary
systems,
and that you keep giving life
even if we do not recognize it.*

*I believe in Jesus of Nazareth,
the human being who rose from the dead by
the power of your love,
who originated in you,
and who always lived and still lives in you,
your son, our brother.
Mary gave birth to him, intimately united with
you,
he died on the cross out of love and
faithfulness for all human beings,
he was buried,
and you awakened him from the dead,
calling him to share eternal life with you.*

I believe in the Holy Spirit,
the creator of love.
I believe that you wish
to change and sanctify our Christian churches,
that you are awaiting our open hearts
so that the earth may remain habitable.

I believe in the community of all those
who seek you under many different names,
for you are divine fullness,
and you wish to heal and gather us together.
I believe that you will unconditionally
accept us as your children,
regardless of whether we are male or female,
black or white, rich or poor.

I believe that you will forgive our sins,
that you will banish sin from our lives,
that you will call us through the tunnel
of death to experience life and joy forever.
Amen.

—Christa Peikert-Flaspöhler

BIBLIOGRAPHY

Since this book was originally published in German, the authors and works quoted in it either were not referenced to English language sources or were translated into English for the first time. The following is a partial list of the identifiable German language sources of their works:

Tilmann Moser, *Gottesvergiftung*, Frankfurt, 1976.

Christa Peikert-Flaspöhler, *Du träumst in mir, mein Gott. Frauen beten*, Topos plus Taschenbuch Nr. 349, Limburg-Kevelaer: Lahn Verlag, 2000.

Karl Rahner and H. Vorgrimler, *Kleines Konzilskompendium*, Freiburg, 1986.

Andrea Schwarz, *Mit Leidenschaft und Gelassenheit*, Freiburg im Breisgau: Verlag Herder, 1995.

Jörg Zink, *Wie wir beten können*, Stuttgart: Kreuz Verlag, 1975.

Karl Frielingsdorf, S.J. is Professor of Pastoral Psychology and Religious Education at the Sankt Georgen Graduate School of Philosophy and Theology in Frankfurt on Main, Germany. He is also Director of the institute for Pastoral Psychology and Spirituality. He is the author of fifteen books, all in German, as well as many articles on theology, psychology, and education.

Other Titles in the Ignatian Impulse Series

The Art of Discernment
Making Good Decisions in Your World of Choices
STEFAN KIECHLE, S.J.

An explanation of the discernment process first developed by St. Ignatius of Loyola. This process involved outlining the pros and the cons, considering what it would be like to live with the decision, listening to our hearts, and seeking the freedom to do what is best.

ISBN: 1-59471-035-X / 128 pages / $9.95
Ave Maria Press

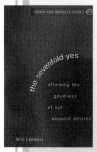

The Sevenfold Yes
Affirming the Goodness of Our Deepest Desires
WILLI LAMBERT, S.J.

The Sevenfold Yes, an affirmation of life's goodness and meaning, is at the very center of the spirituality of St. Ignatius whose motto was to "find God in all things." Prayer exercises and reflection questions help readers recognize God's call in one's heart and the events of everyday life.

ISBN: 1-59471-034-1 / 128 pages / $9.95
Ave Maria Press

Summoned At Every Age
Finding God in Our Later Years
PETER VAN BREEMEN, S.J.

Life summons us at every age—calls us to be ready for new endeavors. Whether in youth or adulthood we are always learning, always growing. Jesuit retreat master Peter van Breemen invites us to recognize that amidst the challenges of growing older there is a profound beauty and grace.

ISBN: 1-59471-036-8 / 128 pages / $9.95
Ave Maria Press

Available at your bookstore, online retailers, or from **ave maria press** at
www.avemariapress.com or 1-800-282-1865. Prices and availablity subject to change.

Keycode: FØAØ1Ø6ØØØØ